'I Didn't Get Where I Am . . .'

'I Didn't Get Where I Am . . .'

HOW THE RICH AND FAMOUS ACHIEVED THEIR SUCCESS

CHARLIE CROKER

First published 2012

The History Press
The Mill, Brimscombe Port
Stroud, Gloucestershire, GL5 2QG
www.thehistorypress.co.uk

British Library Cataloguing in Publication Data.
A catalogue record for this book is available from the British Library.

ISBN 978 0 7524 6531 9

Typesetting and origination by The History Press
Printed in Great Britain

CONTENTS

INTRODUCTION

Did you know that Frederic Chopin slept with wooden wedges between his fingers? Or that Marilyn Monroe often wore shoes with one heel slightly lower than the other? Or that Benjamin Disraeli kept the feet of his bed in bowls of salt?

Without the explanations for *why* they did these things, you might think the three of them were barking mad. But once you learn that Chopin's wedges were to increase the span of his fingers, so allowing him to reach more notes on the piano, his behaviour begins to make sense. Realise that Monroe's unequal heels exacerbated her sexy walk, and you see the habit for the stroke of genius it was. Take on board that Disraeli's salt-bowls were to ward off evil spirits and . . . OK, yes, in that case you are stuck with the conclusion that he was barking mad. Or was he? He did get to be Prime Minister, after all, which is more than you or I have managed. (I'm assuming as I write that you *aren't* a former, or indeed serving, Prime Minister. Call me presumptuous, but I think the odds are in my favour.)

The point is, these insights into the methods (and indeed madness) of the great and the good show us that their greatness and goodness didn't come easily. They *worked* at it. They schemed, planned, connived, hustled, grafted and struggled their way to success. They put some thought into their travails, some cunning into their campaigns. It obviously worked – they're the ones you're reading about in this book, after all. So doesn't it stand to reason that by studying their steps along the road to fame and fortune, you might – as Alf Garnett used to put it – *learn a thing or two?*

Of course you shouldn't fall into the trap of simply copying the tricks and habits contained in these pages. As the Greek philosopher Heraclitus tells us, 'the teaching of many things does not teach understanding.' The French writer Rémy de Gourmont was equally cautious, pointing out that 'to know what everybody else knows is to know nothing.' But as long as you take care to consider what you read here, to assess how it could best be applied to your own life and circumstances, then surely there'll be at least a few tips you can take away? Perhaps it'll be when you read about Margaret Thatcher's way of testing whether her office had been properly cleaned . . . or why Jenson Button sits on an inflatable gym ball before every Grand Prix . . . or the reason Jane Austen wrote on very small pieces of paper. . . .

Whichever bits of the following inspire you to change your own behaviour – indeed even if none of them do – you should, I hope, find them intriguing and sometimes amusing in their own right. You're about to learn how two millennia's worth of high achievers have achieved their heights. You're about to learn the secrets of their success.

Charlie Croker, 2012

GENIUS IS
1% INSPIRATION . . .

Y ou're itching to get started. Fame and fortune
beckon — you just need the idea that's going to do
it for you. Shouldn't take long. Inspiration can't be
that hard, can it? Can it? Er . . .

The question of where ideas come from, and how they can be
accelerated on their journey, has taxed and bedevilled our species'
greatest creative minds since the first caveman fashioned the first
pointy-headed sharp thing and called it a spear. Some pretty great
people have done some pretty weird things in search of that elusive
substance known as 'inspiration'. Beethoven used to tip iced water
over his head as he composed, while Charles II collected dust from
Egyptian mummies and rubbed it on himself to acquire what he termed
'ancient greatness'. Peter Sellers, meanwhile, was inspired by no less
an authority than the Almighty. *'I just talked to God!'* he told director

Blake Edwards one night, after a long day struggling with a difficult scene in a Pink Panther film. *'And he told me how to do it!'* The next day they tried the scene that way – and it was even worse. *'Peter,'* said Edwards, *'next time you talk to God, tell him to stay out of show business.'*

Here's how some other notables have tackled the inspiration issue . . .

Keith Richards often reads the Bible – *'some very good phrases in there'*, he says. He got the title for the Rolling Stones song *Thief in the Night* from Thessalonians 5:2.

Thessalonians 5:2

The Day of the Lord

Now, brothers and sisters, about times and dates we do not need to write to you, for you know very well that the day of the Lord will come like a thief in the night. While people are saying, "Peace and safety," destruction will come on them suddenly, as labor pains on a pregnant woman, and they will not escape.

Stephen Sondheim deliberately improvises in keys he's uncomfortable with, to prevent 'muscle memory' guiding his fingers into tired old patterns.

John Lennon took to composing on piano in the latter part of the Beatles' career precisely because he was unfamiliar with the instrument — it helped to give him fresh ideas.

Albert Einstein did what Sherlock Holmes was famous for – he played the violin as he mused on a problem. He credited it with extending his thinking.

'Not taking risks in art is like not having sex and then expecting there to be children.'

The British comedy writer **John Junkin** was once asked how he inspired himself to write. He said it was very simple: you put a blank sheet of paper in the typewriter, then put the gas bill next to the typewriter.

Alan Bennett says you have to make yourself sit down and try to write something even if you don't immediately feel inspired. He likens it to making yourself go into the post office 'to see if anything's come in.'

Martin Amis: 'You know that foreign correspondent's ruse; in the days when you had your profession on the passport, you put writer; and then when you were in some trouble spot, in order to conceal your identity you simply changed the "r" in writer to an "a" and became a waiter. I always thought there was a great truth there. Writing is waiting, for me certainly. It wouldn't bother me a bit if I didn't write one word in the morning. I'd just think, you know, not yet.'

Douglas Adams: 'Writing is easy. You only need to stare at a piece of blank paper until your forehead bleeds.'

Artist Chuck Close: *'The advice I like to give young artists is not to wait around for inspiration. Inspiration is for amateurs; the rest of us just show up and get to work. If you wait around for the clouds to part and a bolt of lightning to strike you in the brain, you are not going to make an awful lot of work. All the best ideas come out of the process; they come out of the work itself. Things occur to you. If you're sitting around trying to dream up a great art idea, you can sit there a long time before anything happens. But if you just get to work, something will occur to you and something else will occur to you and something else that you reject will push you in another direction. Inspiration is absolutely unnecessary and somehow deceptive. You feel like you need this great idea before you can get down to work, and I find that's almost never the case.'*

Vincent Van Gogh: *'Why should a painter be afraid of a blank canvas? A blank canvas is afraid of the painter; if you take that attitude you've beaten it already.'*

Chris Ofili, the Turner Prize-winning British painter, starts every day by tearing a large sheet of paper into eight pieces, each 6 inches by 9. Then he makes some pencil marks to loosen up: *'they're just a way to say something and nothing with a physical mark that is nothing except a start.'*

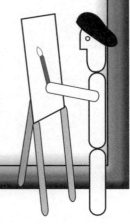

Where inspiration strikes:

The bathroom

Chris Addison: *'I have most of my best ideas when I'm brushing my teeth. Maybe I should floss them, too. One day you'll see me doing an amazing show with really, really clean teeth.'*

Junot Diaz, whose novel *The Brief and Wondrous Life of Oscar Wao* won the Pulitzer Prize, writes in the bathroom, sitting on the edge of the bath.

Hilary Mantel, author of the Booker Prize-winning *Wolf Hall*, counters writer's block by taking a shower.

Demosthenes wrote his speeches after shaving half his head, so that he would be too embarrassed to show himself in public.

The bedroom

Paul McCartney woke up with the tune for 'Yesterday' in his head, and couldn't believe it wasn't an existing song. He had to hum it to several people before being convinced that it was indeed his.

The guitar riff for 'Satisfaction' came to **Keith Richards** in his sleep. The guitarist woke up, recorded the riff and the words 'I can't get no satisfaction' into a cassette recorder, then went back to sleep. Listening back to the tape he heard *'two minutes of "Satisfaction" and 40 minutes of me snoring.'*

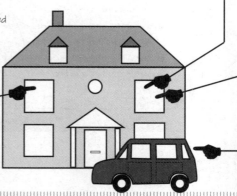

Victor Hugo made himself work by having his valet hide his clothes. He was therefore unable to go out and had no choice but to write – naked.

Samuel Taylor Coleridge dreamed the whole of his poem 'Kubla Khan'. As he wrote it down he was interrupted by a visitor from the village of Porlock, and on resuming found that he couldn't remember any more. This is why the poem stops after just 54 lines. 'A person from Porlock' has come to be literary slang for an unwanted intruder.

Freddie Mercury used a piano as the headboard of his bed. If he awoke with a tune in his head he could reach up behind his head and, being double-jointed, play it straightaway. This is how he composed the beginning of 'Bohemian Rhapsody'.

The car

George Lucas got the inspiration for the Star Wars 'hairy co-pilot' character Chewbacca from his own Alaskan Malamute dog, who used to ride around on the front passenger seat of Lucas' car. The dog – Indiana – also inspired the name of Harrison Ford's character in *Raiders of the Lost Ark*, which Lucas produced. (Meanwhile Lucas got the idea for another Star Wars character while mixing his earlier film *American Graffiti* – he asked the sound engineer for R2-D2, meaning Reel 2 Dialogue 2. Liking the sound of the phrase he noted it down . . .)

Gertrude Stein would sit in her parked Ford car (called Godiva) to write poetry.

The pub

Sebastian Faulks: 'Pub research –
it's quite important to do that.
The difficulty is to determine the
difference between a thought and an idea.
I may be interested in certain notes in a
female singer's repertoire. If I talk about
it in the pub and people's eyes glaze over
and say it's completely uninteresting
then I know it's just a thought I've shared
and move on. But if it lights up their
eyes and they say "yes, I wonder if people
write songs just to include those notes"
and "do you think it's possible a singer
might actually live her life to give herself
material for a song," then suddenly that's
more than a thought, that's an idea.
You can see some sort of flesh on it.'

The importance of routine

Karl Lagerfeld: 'The brain is a muscle and you have to work out not with machines but with your brain. You know, the French say "you get hungry when you are eating" and I think you get ideas when you are working.'

Italian novelist **Alberto Moravia**: 'When I sit at my table to write, I never know what it's going to be till I'm under way. I trust in inspiration, which sometimes comes and sometimes doesn't. But I don't sit back waiting for it. I work every day.'

Somerset Maugham had a very strict routine at his home, the Villa Mauresque on the French Riviera: after breakfast, he would go up to his study at the top of the house, then work from 8.00 a.m. until noon (in longhand). Then he went downstairs and got ready for lunch. He once told a friend that he did that every single day. The friend asked: **'You mean Sundays and holidays and birthdays?'** Maugham replied: **'Especially Sundays and holidays and birthdays.'**

Some notes on notebooks

Francis Bacon (the Elizabethan statesman, not the twentieth-century artist): *'A man would do well to carry a pencil in his pocket, and write down the thoughts of the moment. Those that come unsought are commonly the most valuable, and should be secured, because they seldom return.'* It was advice that Isaac Newton would have approved of – he always had to have a pen in his hand, to help him concentrate. Discretion with your writing implement is important, though. The composer John Cage studied with Schoenberg: *'He pointed out the eraser on his pencil and said, "This end is more important than the other."'*

But of course a pencil is of little use if you've got nothing to write on. This is why the humble notebook has come to be such a crucial tool for so many creative people . . .

Mark Twain used leather-bound notebooks which were custom made to his own design: each page had a tab which could be torn off once the page was full. This allowed Twain to easily find the next blank sheet.

Charles Darwin wrote vertically down the page when out making field notes — he found this the easiest way while holding the book with one hand and writing with the other. He also sometimes started from both ends of the notebook simultaneously and met himself in the middle — a habit he shared with Isaac Newton. Newton numbered the front half with Roman numerals and the back half with Arabic numerals.

Thomas Jefferson's notebook had ivory leaves on which he wrote in pencil. Getting up early every day he would take measurements about the weather, bird migration, plant growth and so on. (He did this wherever he was in the world, using tools he carried with him such as a thermometer, a compass and the like.) Every night he would transfer the results from his notebook to seven large books, each concerned with a different subject. This allowed him to erase the ivory pages, freeing them for use the next day.

Beethoven's notebook was illegible to other people. Wilhelm von Lenz wrote in 1855 that, 'when Beethoven was enjoying a beer he might suddenly pull out his notebook and write something in it. "Something just occurred to me," he would say, sticking it back into his pocket. The ideas that he tossed off separately, with only a few lines and points and without barlines, are hieroglyphics that no one can decipher. Thus in these tiny notebooks he concealed a treasure of ideas.'

When he went deaf, the composer used notebooks as conversation aids. Friends would write down their comments and questions, to which Beethoven could respond orally.

Ernest Hemingway's relationship with his notebook was about as deep as you can get. 'I belong to this notebook and this pencil,' he once declared. He used them in Paris cafés, waiting for inspiration to appear. 'I would stand and look out over the roofs of Paris and think, "Do not worry. You have always written before and you will write now. All you have to do is write one true sentence that you know." So finally I would write one true sentence, and then go on from there. It was easy then because there was always one true sentence that I knew or had seen or had heard someone say.'

Larry David's notebook, according to the comedian's director Robert Weide, is a 'ratty brown thing that looks as if it might have cost forty-nine cents at a stationery store. Its pages are covered with David's illegible scrawl.' A typical instance came when David had no cash for a parking garage valet and had to borrow some from Weide. 'What would I have done if he hadn't been there?' said David. 'That could have been funny.'

David has even written the notebook into his show Curb Your Enthusiasm. He leaves it at a house of a neighbour, who on returning it asks for the $500 reward promised inside the front cover. 'Let me get you a check, Sherlock,' says an angry David.

John D. Rockefeller used a notebook as he toured his oil refineries and processing plants. He would ask questions of the managers, and note down their replies. 'More than once I have gone to luncheon with a number of our heads of departments,' he said, 'and have seen the sweat start out on the foreheads of some of them when that little red notebook was pulled out.'

The nineteenth-century American writer Ralph Waldo Emerson had 263 notebooks, which he indexed in another book of 400 pages. Then he made indexes for specific subjects, and another index for people mentioned in the books. Eventually he even had indexes for his indexes.

Leonardo da Vinci kept tiny (3.5in by 2.5in) notebooks tied to his belt, ready to note down drawings and ideas. His famous 'mirror writing' (from right to left across the page, readable only by viewing it in a mirror) was not so much a secret code as a way of stopping the ink smearing — da Vinci, you see, was left-handed. Though he could, as a party trick, write with both hands simultaneously. US President James Garfield, on the other hand (on the other two hands?), had an even more impressive trick: he could write in Latin with one hand and Greek with the other — again simultaneously.

Sebastian Faulks doesn't carry a notebook to jot down ideas because 'that looks a bit camp. But I do often have cheque books that end up with completely indecipherable scrawls on the back.'

Another solution to that problem came from the American poet Robert Frost — while travelling on a train once he made notes on the sole of his shoe.

Lieutenant Clancey Hatleberg wrote on his clothing for a different reason. He was the US Navy officer who opened up the hatch of Apollo 11 when it landed in the Pacific Ocean after returning from the moon. In charge of ensuring that quarantine conditions were met, he had three main things to remember: make sure the air vent valves on the spacecraft were closed . . . remove the tape from the filters on the astronauts' biological isolation garments . . . and inflate the life preservers on the garments. To ensure he wouldn't forget, as he was helicoptered over to the landing site he wrote across his face mask in red grease pencil: 'Vents, tape, inflate'.

What they listen to in order to inspire them:

SPORTING GREAT: England Rugby World Cup team, 2003

Song	Artist	Notes
'Proud'	M People	Sir Clive Woodward, who coached the team, also draws inspiration from 'Lose Yourself' by Eminem, finding its message (of there being one moment in a lifetime that you have to seize) invaluable in encouraging players.

SPORTING GREAT: England Rugby World Cup team, 2007

Song	Artist	Notes
'The Gambler'	Kenny Rogers	

SPORTING GREAT: Joe Calzaghe

Song	Artist	Notes
'Spitfire'	The Prodigy	Calzaghe had the song played as he came out into the ring for his fights.

SPORTING GREAT: Usain Bolt

Song	Artist	Notes
NONE	NONE	His coach has banned music before he races 'because it might break my concentration'.

SPORTING GREAT: Andy Murray

Song	Artist	Notes
–	Eminem, 50 Cent, Black Eyed Peas	

SPORTING GREAT: Andrew Flintoff

Song	Artist	Notes
'Rocket Man'	Elton John	When the hysteria surrounding the 2005 Ashes series was at its height, Flintoff would listen to the song in the dressing room as a way of blocking out the attention and staying calm.

SPORTING GREAT: the England cricket team

Song	Artist	Notes
'Ring of Fire'	Johnny Cash	The team listened to and sang the song during their 2006 tour of India – that's sportsmen's humour for you . . .

SPORTING GREAT: Natasha Danvers

Song	Artist	Notes
'We Made It'	Busta Rhymes	Britain's bronze medallist in the 2008 Olympics played it constantly when she kept getting injured. *'I would picture myself crossing the line at the Olympics and singing it to my coach in the stands.'*

SPORTING GREAT: Shane Williams

Song	Artist	Notes
'Out of Space', 'Everybody in the Place', 'Breathe' and 'Firestarter'	The Prodigy	The rugby World Player of the Year always plays these same four songs before a match. *'I want something uplifting with a quick beat.'*

The happy accident

The photographer and painter **David Bailey** is a great believer in the happy accident. *'The accident is the thing that makes creativity because if you're painting and a drip goes, you think "S***, I never thought of that drip there."'* In this spirit he always starts working as quickly as possible. *'Pictures don't get better the longer you're around the subject. And you don't want them to be bored with you either because the magic goes. If I go to Delhi, I get off the plane and I start photographing because days later it all starts to look normal.'*

Freddie Mercury's famous short microphone stand came about as the result of a happy accident. A normal stand broke in half during a 1970s gig – deciding he liked it that way, Mercury subsequently had them made specially.

. . . AND 99% PERSPIRATION

Of the three categories listed by **Malvolio** in *Twelfth Night* – 'some are born great, some achieve greatness, some have greatness thrust upon them' – most high-achievers fall into the second category. There are very few true geniuses in this world. And even those who are born with a natural talent have to work hard to improve and maintain it. As Leonardo da Vinci wrote: *'It had long since come to my attention that people of accomplishment rarely sat back and let things happen to them. They went out and happened to things.'* A more modern saying on the subject has come to be associated (for some reason) with the game of golf, being attributed variously to Gary Player and Arnold Palmer. But the original version actually stemmed from Thomas Jefferson: *'I'm a great believer in luck, and I find the harder I work the more I have of it.'*

As **Mark Twain** said, *'the dictionary is the only place where success comes before work.'* You don't have to bust a gut – the American author of motivational books Robert Collier pointed out that *'success is the sum of small efforts, repeated day in and day out'* – but you do have to keep going. *'I walk slowly,'* said Abraham Lincoln. *'But I never walk backward.'* After a while your persistence will become habitual, certainly if you believe Aristotle: *'We are what we repeatedly do.'*

If they felt the need to work hard at achieving success, why shouldn't you?

What does practice make?

Franz Liszt read books while practising piano exercises. But not just any books. *'Poetry interferes subtly with the rhythm of the music, and so does really admirable prose. The most useful, I have found for myself, are detective stories, sociology and literary criticism.'* **Richard Coles**, the classically trained keyboard player with 1980s band The Communards took this habit one stage further: he found the pop parts so simple to perform that during concerts he would keep a book of poetry on top of the keyboard, reading it to prevent himself getting bored.

Fred Astaire practised each dance until he could read a book while performing it.

As a child **Elton John** was forced to practise the piano by his grandmother – although he hated it at the time, he now expresses his gratitude. The young Chopin went to bed with wooden wedges between his fingers, to increase the number of piano keys he could span. Even more extreme measures were employed by **Miles Davis'** childhood trumpet teacher: whenever Davis used vibrato, the teacher would slap his knuckles. Davis grew up to be famous for his vibrato-free sound.

The youthful **Steve Davis** used cheese and Marmite sandwiches as practice incentive – only after potting a set number of balls would he allow himself one. Sometimes he'd use only the white ball, hitting it up and down the table from the brown spot to check that his cue action was straight. The regulars in his club laughed at this eccentricity – until he became successful, after which they formed his entourage at tournaments, known as the 'Romford Mafia'.

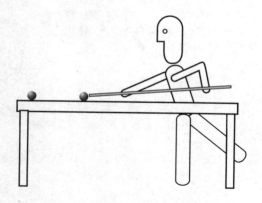

As a child **Donald Bradman** practised batting by hitting a golf ball with a cricket stump. He would hit the ball against a curved brick wall, from which it would rebound at differing angles — then try to hit it again.

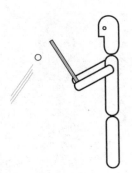

Before every Grand Prix **Jenson Button** sits on an inflatable gym ball, holding a steering wheel. He then shuts his eyes and drives an imaginary lap of the circuit, making all the appropriate noises. He invariably finishes the lap within a second of his real time.

In the 2011 Rugby World Cup, knowing that heavy rain was forecast for England's match against Scotland, **Jonny Wilkinson** practised kicking with rugby balls that had been soaked in water. There was indeed torrential rain during the match. Wilkinson scored two penalties and a drop goal, helping England to win the match.

If you're determined to be lazy, though, there are one or two precedents you can follow. **Buddy Rich**, often cited as the greatest drummer ever, claimed never to practise. He also said he had never had a lesson — it would have diminished his talent. Three-time World Professional Snooker Champion **Fred Davis** also shunned the practice of practice; he believed you should save your best shots for competition.

Attention to detail

Thomas Carlyle once said that *'genius is an infinite capacity for taking pains'*. The spellbinding eureka moment, when everything falls into place in a single ecstatic flash of revelation, is very much the exception to a rather mundane norm. Most big achievements are made up lots of little ones, all of them sweated over, all of them fiddly, and none of them amounting to very much in themselves. It's in the determination to carry on sweating and fiddling, and then to join all your little achievements together, that true greatness is to be found.

The music producer **Quincy Jones** always has a small speaker on the mixing desk which recreates how a song will sound when played on the radio. Listening to what was going to be the final mix of Michael Jackson's *Thriller* through this speaker, he realised that weeks and weeks of work had failed to produce a sufficiently impressive album. So he insisted on stripping every track down to its constituent parts, and remixing them all until he was satisfied. *Thriller* went on to become the biggest-selling album in history.

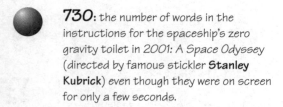

730: the number of words in the instructions for the spaceship's zero gravity toilet in *2001: A Space Odyssey* (directed by famous stickler **Stanley Kubrick**) even though they were on screen for only a few seconds.

500: the number of sittings that **Cézanne** would sometimes take to complete a portrait.

115: the number of sittings for one portrait after which **Cézanne** destroyed it. The best he could say of it was, '*I am not entirely displeased with the shirt front.*'

3: the number of hours director **Vincente Minnelli** kept an actress in a bubble bath while shooting *Yolanda and the Thief*, because he needed to perfect the background details that could be seen through the angle of her arm as she answered a telephone.

60: The speed in miles per hour at which, according to one review of a new Rolls-Royce, the loudest thing was the clock. Reading this review, the firm's chief engineer said, '*it's time we did something about that damned clock.*'

George Mair, a journalist for the *Guardian* in the days when it was still known as the *Manchester Guardian*, prompted a colleague to remark (admiringly) that Mair '*once telephoned a semi-colon from Moscow.*'

On the set of *The West Wing*, there was even stationery *inside* the desk drawers.

Coping with other people's perfectionism can be a skill in itself. **Enn Reitel**, one of the most successful British voiceover artists ever, once did a session down the line for an American company. After several takes the chief executive in the States gave an instruction along the lines of 'now could we try one where you stress the third word more, but not as much as you did in take seven . . .' Reitel and the engineer said 'of course', then played the chief executive a recording of their last take. *'That's great,'* came the reply. *'Just what we needed.'*

Sometimes the skill is in knowing which details *not* to worry about. Ted Tally, who wrote the screenplay for *The Silence of the Lambs*, refers to 'refrigerator questions', giving as an example the fact that Hannibal Lecter couldn't possibly have known the number of the payphone on which he dials Clarice Starling at the end of the film. *'You've seen the movie, you've enjoyed it, you get home and open the refrigerator and say "wait a minute! How could that guy have done that?" If it doesn't occur to you until you get to the refrigerator, it's not important enough for us to worry about.'*

'I re-wrote the ending to Farewell to Arms, the last page of it, thirty-nine times before I was satisfied.'

'Was there some technical problem there? What was it that had stumped you?'

'Getting the words right.'

HEMINGWAY   INTERVIEWER

It was an approach Hemingway stuck to. His son Patrick once asked him to edit a story he'd written. Hemingway duly did so. **'But, Papa,'** Patrick said, **'you've only changed one word.' 'If it's the right word,'** came the reply, **'that's a lot.'**

Keith Richards gets even more detailed than individual words – he concentrates on individual vowel sounds. He'll know instinctively that a certain word in a particular line should have, say, an 'oo' or an 'ee' sound, and will work backwards from there to find a word that fits. He calls this approach to lyric-writing 'vowel movement'.

American football quarterback **Don Meredith** on legendary Dallas Cowboys coach Tom Landry: *'He was such a perfectionist, if he was married to Raquel Welch he'd expect her to cook.'*

Knowing your own mind

Dustin Hoffman: *'I'd like to reach a point where I no longer bullshit myself. I think that's the natural human condition – to lie to yourself. Because the truth is painful.'*

David Lean: *'I wouldn't take the advice of a lot of so-called critics on how to shoot a close-up of a teapot.'*

Alfred Hitchcock: *'When an actor comes to me and wants to discuss his character, I say, "It's in the script". If he says, "But what's my motivation?" I say "Your salary".'*

Terry Gilliam: 'Dear Sid Sheinberg, When are you going to release my film Brazil? Terry Gilliam.' (as worded in a full page ad in Variety magazine when the studio boss refused to release Gilliam's preferred version)*

Bruce Lee always refused to chop boards in half with his hand, saying that it wasn't what martial arts were about: 'There's no challenge in breaking a board. Boards don't hit back.'

'I cannot give you the formula for success, but I can give you the formula for failure – which is: try to please everybody.' Herbert Bayard Swope (Pulitzer Prize-winning US editor and journalist)

*The US critics, who were on Gilliam's side (he'd organised illicit screenings of the film), discovered that a movie didn't have to be released for it to be eligible for a Los Angeles Film Critics Association award – so they gave it Best Picture, Best Screenplay and Best Director, forcing the studio to release it.

It's not what you know . . . or is it?

'The secret of success is to know something nobody else knows.' Aristotle Onassis

'As a general rule the most successful man in life is the man who has the best information.'
Benjamin Disraeli

Two different views of how to be specific in your strategy:

British comedian **Chris Addison**:
'Make your Plan B as unfeasible as possible. That should encourage Plan A.'

Thomas Edison set himself a target of one minor invention every 10 days and a major one every 6 months.

The power of persistence

How many times they were rejected before finding a publisher:

J.K. Rowling's first *Harry Potter* book: 12

John Grisham's first novel *A Time to Kill*   12

Richard Adams' *Watership Down*:   13

Anne Frank's *Diary of a Young Girl*:   15

William Golding's *Lord of the Flies*:   20

Frank Herbert's *Dune*:   23

Dr Seuss' first novel *To Think That I*
  Saw It On Mulberry Street: 27

Stephen King's first novel *Carrie*:   30
  (at which point he threw it in the bin – his wife
  fished it out and told him to keep submitting it)

Marina Lewycka's *A Short History of*
  Tractors in Ukrainian: 36

Margaret Mitchell's *Gone with the Wind*:   38

Robert Pirsig's *Zen and the Art of*
  Motorcycle Maintenance: 121

Jack Canfield and **Mark Victor Hansen's** *Chicken*
  Soup for the Soul: 140

Jack London before his first novel was published: 600

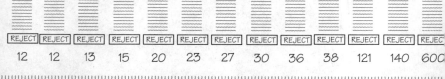

REJECT	REJECT	REJECT	REJECT	REJECT	REJECT	REJECT	REJECT	REJECT	REJECT	REJECT	REJECT	REJEC
12	12	13	15	20	23	27	30	36	38	121	140	600

Michael Caine has adopted Churchill's motto:
'when you're going through hell, keep going.'

Once, when **John Singer Sargent** lost faith in his own abilities, he made himself continue with a painting of some roses until his confidence returned. Although critics loved the painting he always refused to sell it, preferring to keep it as a reminder of the need to work through difficult times.

In some circumstances persistence takes on a very physical – and painful – form. During the 1975 Dutch Grand Prix, the top of **James Hunt**'s gearstick came off, leaving nothing but a sharp piece of metal sticking up. Every change of gear for the rest of the race meant sticking his increasingly bloodied palm onto that piece of metal and jerking the stick into position. But Hunt did it, and eventually came out the winner – his first Grand Prix victory.

1 performance at the Grand Ole Opry in Nashville by Elvis Presley before he was fired by the manager Jimmy Denny, who told him: *'You ain't goin' nowhere, son. You ought to go back to drivin' a truck.'*

3 rejections from the University of Southern California School of Theater, Film and Television for a young Steven Spielberg.

7 failed businesses started by R.H. Macy before he opened his iconic New York store.

Fewer than 100 rice cookers sold by Akio Morita (the invention burned rice rather than cooked it) — undeterred, Morita went on to found Sony.

1,009 rejections for Harland David Sanders' chicken recipe before a restaurant accepted it, leading to 'Colonel' Sanders and his Kentucky Fried Chicken chain.

1,330 strikeouts by legendary baseball player Babe Ruth, who is more famous for his 714 home runs. For many decades, in fact, he held the record for the number of strikeouts. It never bothered him. *'Every strike brings me closer to the next home run.'*

9,000+ shots missed by Michael Jordan. *'I have lost almost 300 games. On 26 occasions I have been entrusted to take the game-winning shot, and I missed. I have failed over and over and over again in my life. And that is why I succeed.'*

10,000 failed attempts by Thomas Edison at producing a storage battery. Not that he saw it this way. *'Why, I have not failed. I've just found 10,000 ways that won't work.'* His overall philosophy was summed up as: *'Our greatest weakness lies in giving up. The most certain way to succeed is always to try just one more time.'*

Keeping it simple

Just because you're working hard doesn't mean that that work has to be complicated. Remember the lessons of these greats who kept things simple:

Alfred Hitchcock: *'To make a great film you need three things – the script, the script and the script.'*

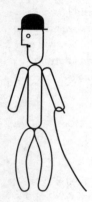

Charlie Chaplin: *'I remain just one thing, and one thing only, and that is a clown. It places me on a far higher plane than any politician.'*

Francis Rossi, on criticism of Status Quo for only using three chords: *'What, you mean three chords and a crap melody or three chords and a great one? I mean, 'Nessun Dorma', the main part's three chords, and 'La Donna e Mobile', that's three chords . . .'* Rossi also points out that no one ever *'goes up to Mr Coca or Mr Cola and says, you know how you've been really successful with that recipe of yours – why don't you try changing it?'*

Ted Guillory, lead flight planner for the Apollo 11 mission that took Neil Armstrong and Buzz Aldrin to the moon, regularly used little drawings in the crew's instructions. *'See here, what is this "pitch 180, roll 180 and pitch 322"? That's all nice, but here you drew a picture and that was the way the spacecraft should be with respect to the moon. Sometimes the simple things that you don't have a big computer program for turn out to be the most useful of all.'*

Irving Berlin never learned to play in more than one key. If he needed to play in a different one he used a custom-made Weser Brothers piano with a transposing lever that changed keys for him.

Resisting the temptation to over-complicate your work can sometimes require outside help. **Sting** has said of albums what Truman Capote once said of novels: you never feel as though they're finished, there just comes a stage when people take them away from you.

Also, remember that what *looks* simple can often take a long time to achieve. **Mark Twain** was once sent a telegram by a publisher: *'Need 2-page short story 2 days'*. Twain replied: *'No can do 2 pages 2 days. Can do 30 pages 2 days. Need 30 days to do 2 pages.'*

Sharp elbows

Excessively pointy joints in the middle of your arms might not be the most attractive feature, but you have to remember that all that work on improving your chances of success might not be enough. Someone else is working on improving *their* chances of success. And sometimes the stage ain't big enough for the both of you.

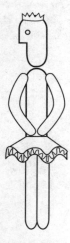

In the 1989 film *Batman* the British actor **Richard Strange** appeared as a member of the gang led by the Joker, played by Jack Nicholson. In rehearsals for the scene where they trash an art gallery, Strange found himself standing before a picture of a ballerina. Improvising, he did a pirouette, then smashed the picture. When it came to the first take Strange, before he could repeat the joke, watched Nicholson perform exactly the same move.

On the day of Live Aid **Cher** found herself on the same Concorde flight as **Phil Collins**, who was travelling between the London and Philadelphia legs of the event in order to perform at both. Quite where Cher had been for the previous few weeks isn't clear, but she'd somehow managed to hear absolutely nothing at all about the concert. Once Collins had explained to her what was going on — and how many people were watching — she asked if he could get her onto the bill. That night she was seen by a worldwide audience, singing along on the Philadelphia stage in the 'We are the World' finale.

Meanwhile back at the London leg of Live Aid, Queen stole the show with a mesmerising set that wowed everyone in Wembley Stadium. The days of rehearsal they put in for the gig (at the capital's Shaw Theatre) are well-known – but we shouldn't forget the role of their sound engineer who, under the pretence of 'just having a look' at the sound desk, sneakily switched off the sound limiters. As the band's drummer **Roger Taylor** has said, one reason they were better than anyone else at Live Aid was that *'we were louder than anyone else at Live Aid'*.

And if you think that some talents are so huge their owners don't need sharp elbows, listen to **John Lennon**: *'Things are left out, about what bastards we were. You have to be a bastard to make it, and that's a fact. And the Beatles are the biggest bastards on earth.'*

Worried that people will remember how you used your sharp elbows? You shouldn't be – as Elizabeth Taylor put it: *'Success is a great deodorant. It takes away all your past smells.'*

And finally . . .

If in doubt, get stuck in. As Samuel Beckett put it: *'Try again. Fail again. Fail better.'* Or if you prefer Henry Ford: *'When everything seems to be going against you, remember that the airplane takes off against the wind, not with it.'* Ford's first vehicle – the Quadricycle, equipped with four bicycle tyres – was built in a workshop. No problem with the vehicle as such, it was just too big to get out of the workshop's door. Ford never doubted himself, though. *'Whether you think you can or whether you think you can't,'* he said, *'you're right.'*

Others who kept at it in spite of early failure:

F.W. Woolworth: the young Woolworth worked at a dry goods store, where the boss forbade him from talking to customers, as he didn't have the skill to do so.

Soichiro Honda: was turned down by the Toyota Motor Corporation as an engineer. He started his own firm instead. *'Success,'* he would say later, *'is ninety-nine per cent failure.'*

Bill Gates: dropped out of Harvard, started a business called Traf-O-Data. It failed. Started another one called Microsoft.

Walt Disney: sacked by a newspaper editor because he 'lacked imagination and had no good ideas.'

Charles Schultz: rejected by (ahem) Walt Disney's company – went on to create the Peanuts comic strip.

Albert Einstein: didn't speak until he was four, didn't read until he was seven. Expelled from school, rejected by Zurich Polytechnic School. (It's said – and surely this is apocryphal – that Einstein's first words were at the dinner table: *'The soup is too hot.'* His astonished parents asked why he'd never spoken before. *'Because up until now,'* came the reply, *'everything was in order.'*)

Jerry Seinfeld: the first time he walked on stage at a comedy club, Seinfeld froze, and was booed off. He went back the next night, conquered his fear and got laughs with his set.

Fred Astaire: the testing director at MGM wrote after Astaire's first screen test: *'Can't act. Can't sing. Slightly bald. Can dance a little.'* Astaire kept the note for the rest of his life.

Sidney Poitier: the casting director at Poitier's first audition said: *'Why don't you stop wasting people's time and go out and become a dishwasher or something?'*

Dick Rowe: the Decca record executive is most famous for having rejected the Beatles on the grounds that 'guitar groups are on the way out' – but it's often forgotten that he learned from the mistake, and went on to sign another group called the Rolling Stones.

THE 'WOW' FACTOR

Creating an impression

So much of our success in life – or lack of it – depends on how others see us. *'Star quality,'* as Jack Nicholson puts it, *'is if you're on stage and a cat walks on, they still watch you.'* You might think that you're either born with that quality or you're not. That there's no point trying to achieve it. But listen to that same Hollywood star talking about himself: *'With my sunglasses on, I'm Jack Nicholson. Without them, I'm fat and seventy.'* There's always something you can do, some trick you can learn, some effort you can make to subtly – or maybe even radically – improve the impression you make on other people.

Dress to impress

Jerry Lewis would never sit down in his stage tuxedo — he didn't want it to get creased.

Eric Clapton used to have leather pads sewn into the right shoulder of his Armani suits to protect the material from his guitar strap.

Beau Brummel spent two hours washing and dressing every morning. He polished his boots (including the soles) using champagne froth. But he was wary of preparation that showed, saying that if a man was noticed for his clothes, he was overdressed.

Charles I wore two shirts for his execution — it was a cold January day, and he was worried that if he shivered the crowd would mistake it for fear.

Alfred Hitchcock always wore a suit and tie on his film sets.

Frank Sinatra said a hat should always be cocked. *'Angles,'* he said, *'are attitudes.'*

Edgar Allan Poe got there before Johnny Cash by always wearing black, while American poet Emily Dickinson was the forerunner of reporter-turned-politician Martin Bell and cricket commentator Richie Benaud by always wearing white. Another fan of white was Mark Twain. He wore shirts (designed by himself) that buttoned down the back.

Nick Davies, the *Guardian* journalist who did much to break the 2011 'phone hacking' story, always wears a particular shade of pale blue shirt when he goes to doorstep people, as it makes them more amenable to being interviewed. (He also makes a point of never parking right outside their house — he leaves his car down the road and walks to their door.)

Sometimes your clothing is about how you feel, rather than those you meet. TV and radio presenter Gabby Logan has a superstition that when she hosts a show for the first time she always wears red underwear.

Impressing by numbers

500: Cary Grant: *'It takes 500 small details to add up to one favourable impression.'*

67: **Roman Emperor** Augustus' height in inches — he wore shoes with heavy soles to make himself appear taller.

1: The number of strings that could be left on a violin and **Niccolò Paganini** still be able to play it. He would sometimes deliberately play with pre-frayed strings so that they would break, leaving him able to show off with the last remaining one.

2: As if to show the value of brevity, **Alfred Hitchcock** delivered the shortest acceptance speech in the history of the Oscars. Collecting his 1967 honorary award, he said simply: *'thank you'*.

The gift of the gab

When speaking in public, Charles Dickens always insisted on a maroon table, maroon screen and maroon carpet.

Bill Deedes typed his speeches in short segments, like the stanzas of a poem, so that he could read them easily without having to constantly look at the page.

BBC 5 Live interviewer Richard Bacon: *'When I've asked all my questions, I re-ask the questions I asked earlier, but in a slightly different way. No one seems to notice.'*

Churchill constantly tried to eliminate his speech impediment, practising the phrase *'the Shpanish ships I cannot shee for they are not in shite.'* He was also unafraid to borrow from others: 'blood, toil, tears and sweat' was first used by Theodore Roosevelt in 1897.
F.E. Smith said of his friend Churchill: *'He has devoted the best years of his life to preparing his impromptu speeches.'*

From the memoirs of Walter Thompson, Churchill's bodyguard: *'He not only composed but he acted every line . . . He would rap out words, emphasising a climax with a sudden gesture. Now and again he would throw up his arms. Suddenly his voice would break at the emotion he put into his words and tears would pour down his cheeks . . . He would come to a part, which was meant to be humorous, and he would chuckle. He lived every moment.'* He insisted on silent typewriters so that his secretaries could put his dictation straight onto the page without the sound of keys disturbing his flow.

60: number of minutes' preparation that Churchill undertook for every one minute of a speech.

Longer doesn't always equal better when it comes to public speaking. In 1863 **Edward Everett** spoke for 2 hours at the dedication ceremony of a new Soldiers' National Cemetery in Pennsylvania, USA. But no one remembers the speech, or indeed his name. What they remember is the speech delivered straight afterwards, which contained only 272 words. The speaker was Abraham Lincoln, and the exact location of the cemetery was Gettysburg – yes, the Gettysburg Address was a mere 2 minutes long.

Nineteenth-century Prime Minister, Lord Palmerston, responded to bad reactions to a speech by gathering journalists together and dictating a new one. The obedient press would report this as though it had been the real speech.

Talking in a court of law is a very particular skill. The writer **John Mortimer**, who started his career as a barrister, tried learning from his father, who had followed the same profession. Mortimer Senior always counted up to ten in his head before asking his first question, to gain everyone's attention. Trying the same thing, his son was told to hurry up by the judge: **'We can't all sit here watching you standing in silent prayer, you know.'** So Mortimer switched to copying another advocate, Cyril Salmon, who would stroll nonchalantly up and down, playing with a gold watch chain as he calmly cross-examined witnesses. **'Do keep still,'** said a judge when Mortimer tried it. **'It's like watching ping pong.'**

The TV cookery presenter **John Torode** was told by his father: **'Son, always blow your own trumpet, because otherwise someone will use it as a spittoon.'** Years later, when Torode had his own London restaurant and took his father to the top floor, the response was: **'Call that a view? Where's the bloody water?'**

John Motson: *'I used to get nervous before games and have sleepless nights. Then Rod Stewart invited me to his football pitch in Essex and I asked him if he felt the same before going on stage. Rod said, "Why should I be nervous, singing is what I do." And I thought, commentating is what I do.'*

Margaret Thatcher warns us to be wary of oratory for its own sake: *'In politics, if you want anything said ask a man. If you want something done, ask a woman.'*

Body language

To help him cry on film, **Michael Caine** has a very sad incident from his past that he recalls – he refuses to tell anyone, even his wife, what it is.

Prime Minister **Harold Wilson**'s famous pipe was just to create a 'man of the people' image – in private he smoked cigars.

Adolf Hitler was convinced that people's hands told you a great deal about them. He had a book containing pictures of the hands of famous people, and would show guests how closely his own hands resembled those of his hero Frederick the Great.

'When the eyes say one thing, and the tongue another, a practiced man relies on the language of the first.' Ralph Waldo Emerson

Roger Taylor says that Queen's approach to the first 10 minutes of a gig was very simple: *'blind 'em and deafen 'em.'*

While giving evidence to the Foreign Affairs Select Committee at the House of Commons in the aftermath of the Iraq invasion, **Alastair Campbell** held a paper clip in his hand. Whenever he was in danger of losing his temper he dug the clip's sharp point into his palm, using the pain to distract him. Similarly, David Tennant digs his fingernails into his palms when acting to stop himself either laughing or crying inappropriately. He got the trick not from Campbell but from Esther Rantzen, who did it to stop herself crying during stories on *That's Life*.

When the 12-year-old **Diego Maradona** worked as a ball boy for the Argentinos Juniors team in Buenos Aires, he showed off his astounding skills at half time to get himself noticed by the crowd.

Creating publicity

The American press agent **Harry Reichenbach** (1882–1931) is seen by many as the man who invented the Hollywood publicity stunt. When *The Return of Tarzan* was released, he hired an actor to check into a hotel under the name Thomas R. Zann. A huge crate was delivered to Zann's room (it had to be hoisted through the window), and then 15lbs of raw beef was ordered from room service. An astonished member of staff entered the room to find a pet lion. The police were called – publicity ensued . . .

Reichenbach convinced his client Rudolf Valentino to grow a beard purely because everyone would dislike it, allowing Valentino to earn good publicity from shaving it off.

Another client was Francis X. Bushman. Reichenbach walked him from Grand Central station in New York to Metro Pictures' office, dropping coins from his pocket as he went. People started following them to collect the coins, meaning that when they reached the office Bushman had a huge crowd around him. Metro signed the actor up.

A couple of decades later, a young **Dean Martin** and **Jerry Lewis** created their own publicity while appearing in Atlantic City. Copying a stunt W.C. Fields had once used there, Lewis would wade out into the sea, then pretend to have got into difficulty. Martin would 'rescue' him, lie him down on the sand, then just as he was about to administer mouth-to-mouth, Lewis would sit bolt upright and say *'I'd rather have a malted, sir!'*

Martin: *'We're fresh out.'* Then: *'Hey, don't I know you?'*

Lewis: *'I'm Jerry Lewis!'*

Martin: *'And I'm Dean Martin!'*

Lewis: *'I know that – I'm at the 500 Club with you, first show is at eight o'clock!'*

Think of your audience

They're the ones who attend your gigs, buy your products, see your films. Take them for granted and you'll soon regret it . . .

Louis Armstrong: 'My life has always been my music, it's always come first, but the music ain't worth nothing if you can't lay it on the public. The main thing is to live for that audience, 'cause what you're there for is to please the people.'

Steven Spielberg, on *Jaws*: 'When my mechanical shark was being repaired and I had to shoot something, I had to make the water scary. I relied on the audience's imagination, aided by where I put the camera. Today, it would be a digital shark. It would cost a hell of a lot more, but never break down. As a result, I probably would have

used it four times as much, which would have made the film four times less scary. Jaws is scary because of what you don't see, not because of what you do. We need to bring the audience back into partnership with storytelling.'

Alfred Hitchcock knew the value of a trademark, in his case the habit of making cameo appearances in his own movies. He also knew that a trademark can get in the way – after a while he deliberately made his appearances at the beginning of films, because he knew the audience would be looking for him and he didn't want to divert their attention from the plot.

Hitchcock constantly saw his movies through the eyes of his audience, saying that **'the length of a film should be directly related to the endurance of the human bladder'** and that 'a good film is when the price of the dinner, the theatre admission and the babysitter were worth it.'

The nineteenth-century concert pianist **Vladimir de Pachmann** became famous for his incessant tinkering with the piano stool before beginning his recitals. Asked by a British journalist why he did this, he replied: **'I play to English public on Sunday afternoons. On Sunday, English people eat splendid luncheon. They are like lions – they like to sleep when they are full. I don't like to play to people who fall asleep. So I invent my own technique. I play foolish tricks. I make them laugh at Crazy Old Pachmann until I am sure they are awake. Then I begin my concert.'**

One exception to the 'think of your audience' rule was the late Steve Jobs. Asked what market research had gone into developing the iPad, he replied: **'None. It's not the consumers' job to know what they want.'**

A colourful thought

David Bailey prefers his photographs to be in black and white: *'Black and white gives you the message immediately. Colour's a warning thing. Berries are red so that the birds know to eat them. When they're green they don't eat them. When you look at a colour picture you see the colour before you see the message.'*

The name game

Rock Hudson

was born Roy Scherer, but his agent Henry Wilson came up with the stage name by combining the Rock of Gibraltar with the Hudson River

Paul Hewson

got the name Bono from a hearing aid shop called Bonavox, which literally means 'good voice'

John Cleese's

father changed the family surname from Cheese because he did not want them to be laughed at

Ralph Lauren

was originally Ralph Lifshitz

Mel Blanc

the voice of Bugs Bunny, changed his surname from Blank after a schoolteacher said that's all his life was ever going to be

Whoopi Goldberg

was born Caryn Elaine Johnson – her mother recommended the new surname because Johnson wasn't 'Jewish enough' for her to become a star. 'Whoopi', however, was less calculated: it was a nickname that came from her habitual flatulence

Nicolas Cage

is really Nicolas Coppola – the nephew of Godfather director Francis Ford Coppola, he changed his name to avoid accusations of nepotism

Cary Grant:

'I have spent the greater part of my life fluctuating between Archie Leach and Cary Grant, unsure of each, suspecting each.'

Tim Martin

took the name JD Wetherspoon for his pub chain from one of his old teachers (one who couldn't keep control of his class)

George Harrison

got the idea for the name of the song 'Handle with Care' when he saw it written on an instrument packing case in the studio

Marc Bolan

(originally Mark Feld) took his stage surname from the first two letters of **Bo**b and the last two of Dy**lan**

Nelson Mandela

was born Rolihlahla Mandela – the change was in tribute to Horatio Nelson and is thanks to his schoolteacher who gave English names to all her pupils

Impressing your opponents

Christopher Columbus, knowing that an eclipse was due, told Jamaicans that he would make the moon disappear if they didn't sell him the provisions he wanted. When the eclipse happened they quickly gave way.

Duncan Goodhew found himself in the final of the 100 metres breaststroke at the 1976 Olympics. 40 minutes before the race the eight competitors were put in a 'holding room', a small glass room (they could see out, but no one could see in) where they watched the preceding races on TV. *'All this,'* he says, *'amid the most profound silence you've ever heard in your life. I was completely and utterly overwhelmed. Deep inside myself I questioned my right to be there.'* Goodhew came second to last. Four years later, he deliberately spent his time in the holding area reading a Wilbur Smith novel. *'The best tactic with opponents, especially Russians, is to ignore their presence completely. They really got upset when I did that. I had no idea we were even about to start until an official came and took the book away.'* Goodhew duly won the gold medal.

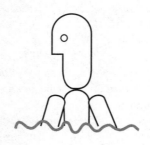

Impressing potential employers

An ex-BBC radio producer says that the actress **Miriam Margolyes** used to stand in the main corridor of the drama department and shout: *'Have any of you arseholes got some work for a fat old dyke?'*

Impressing the little people

Elvis had 20 copies of his gun licence made so officials could take one each.

Frank Sinatra gave away $50,000 dollars' worth of gold cigarette lighters before he was 30. His concern for 'unimportant' people also showed when a young woman at a party he was giving accidentally smashed one of a pair of ornamental birds. The room fell silent. *'Oh,'* cried Sinatra's daughter, *'that was one of my mother's favourite ...'* Sinatra cut her off, then walked over, knocked the other bird off the table, put an arm round the woman and said *'that's OK, kid.'*

To protect his chances of re-election as an MP, **Clement Freud** used to monitor the births, deaths and marriages columns in his constituency newspaper, and write to everyone concerned, offering congratulations or commiserations as appropriate. Often they would approach him in the street, thanking him for the taking the trouble, which put him in the awkward position of not knowing what the letter had been about. He eventually thought up a catch-all reply: **'It was the least I could do.'**

Impressing the big people

Cleopatra showed Antony how wealthy she was by dropping a pearl earring into her drink, so letting it dissolve to nothing.

In 1977 the London advertising agency Allen, Brady and Marsh were invited to bid for the British Railways contract. The chairman of BR, Sir Peter Parker, arrived at ABM's offices to hear their pitch. He was ignored for several minutes by a very-bored looking receptionist. When she finally deigned to speak to him, she told Parker to take a seat in a revoltingly filthy reception area, where half-empty plastic coffee cups sat next to overflowing ashtrays. Half an hour passed, during which there was no sign of ABM's head Peter Marsh. Eventually Parker stood up and headed for the door, seeing no reason to waste any more time on this disrespectful firm. Only then did Marsh appear, uttering the line: **'This is what your customers have to put with every day – let's see how we can put it right.'** ABM won the contract.

Also in the world of advertising — when the **Saatchi** brothers started their agency in London and had a client visiting, they would pay people from the street outside a fiver to come and sit at desks, pretending to be employees.

In 1519, the Italian banker **Agostino Chigi** held a series of dinners at his villa in Rome for the Pope. Twenty foreign cardinals were in attendance, all of whom were served food and wine that had been brought in specially from their home countries. Chigi, who at 40 was the richest man in Rome, had more silver and gold plate than the rest of the city's nobility put together. At the end of each course, rather than use the same silver platters again, he ordered his guests to throw them into the River Tiber.

The next morning someone saw Chigi's servants pulling up nets from the bottom of the river to recover the platters.

Don't believe your own hype

You've got to take your job seriously — but don't ever take yourself too seriously:

Robert Duvall says that between takes on The Godfather the actors used to moon each other.

David Dimbleby: *'Before a broadcast starts, I sometimes tell myself: it's all right, don't worry, this time tomorrow you'll be at home. But the moment I start, there's no broadcast I've done that I haven't enjoyed. In fact, the worse things get, the more fun I have.'*

Ralph Richardson: *'Acting is merely the art of keeping a large group of people from coughing.'*

In 1966 **Bob Dylan** was asked by an interviewer from *Playboy* magazine what his songs were about. *'Oh,'* he replied, *'some are about four minutes, some are about five and some, believe it or not, are about eleven or twelve.'*

John Cleese: *'Probably one of the reasons I've been successful at my kind of acting is that I was entirely self-taught. Everyone in America assumes that we [the Monty Python team] were all at drama schools or studying theatre at university – but not a single one of us ever had a lesson.'*

His colleague Michael Palin has never taken anything too seriously: *'I always felt that civilised behaviour was generally on a knife-edge. I remember feeling that at school assemblies. Someone would get up there and start talking, and I'd think "if a man on a length of wire, stark naked, suddenly swung across the stage, what would happen? What would happen if I ran up there and stuffed a banana in his face?" These people are all playing a game, being terribly straight and focused.'*

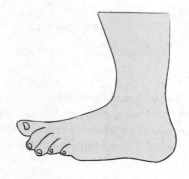

GET YOUR
STRENGTH UP

Sleeping and eating

'Laugh and the world laughs with you,' said Anthony Burgess,
'snore and you sleep alone.' Meanwhile another author, Jane Austen,
commented that *'good apple pies are a considerable part of our
domestic happiness.'* You're not going to get very far in life if you don't
feel rested or well-fed. Here's how some of the great and good down
the ages have slept and eaten . . .

Sleeping

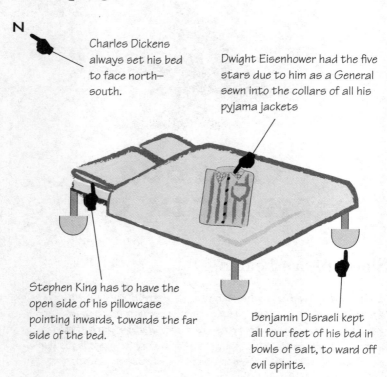

N

Charles Dickens always set his bed to face north–south.

Dwight Eisenhower had the five stars due to him as a General sewn into the collars of all his pyjama jackets

Stephen King has to have the open side of his pillowcase pointing inwards, towards the far side of the bed.

Benjamin Disraeli kept all four feet of his bed in bowls of salt, to ward off evil spirits.

How much shut-eye?

	Hours sleep per night				
	1	2	3	4	5
Margaret Thatcher	ZZZZZZZZZZZZZZZZZ				
Donald Trump	ZZZZZZZZZZZZZZZZZ				
Martha Stewart	ZZZZZZZZZZZZZZZZZZZ				
Barack Obama	ZZZZZZZZZZZZZZZZZZZ				

But Obama still doesn't start work until 9.00 a.m. – two hours later than his predecessor George W. Bush. Though even Dubya seems like a slacker compared to Catherine the Great: she rose at 5.00 a.m. each day.

Mary Higgins Clark started writing at 5.00 a.m. each day, while Sylvia Plath was even earlier, starting at 4.00 a.m. They each did it because with young children it was the only time they could find.

Benjamin Franklin rose each morning at 5 o'clock and asked himself *'What good shall I do today?'* He went to bed each night at 10, asking *'What good have I done today?'*

John Paul Getty: *'Formula for success: Rise early, work hard, strike oil.'*

Routine matters

Honoré de Balzac:

Midnight	get up, start work
Dawn	bathe for 1 hour (copying Napoleon), then recommence work
Lunchtime	sandwich or an egg, recommence work
5.00 p.m.	dinner, see friends
8.00 p.m.	go to bed

Winston Churchill:

8.00 a.m.	wake, breakfast, read mail and all national newspapers, work, dictating to secretaries – all conducted in bed*
11.00 a.m.	rise, take bath, drink a weak whisky and soda
1.00 p.m.	lunch (with a 1-pint bottle of Pol Roger champagne, port, brandy and cigars)
3.30 p.m.	work in study/supervise work on his estate
5.00 p.m.	another whisky and soda, take nap (he said this siesta, a habit learned in Cuba, let him work 36 hours in every 24**)
6.30 p.m.	wake, another bath
8.00 p.m.	dinner
11.00 p.m.	more work until the small hours

Franz Kafka:

8.30 a.m. to 2.30 p.m.	day job at the Workers' Accident Insurance Institute
2.30 p.m. – 3.30 p.m.	lunch
3.30 p.m. – 7.00 p.m.	sleep
7.00 p.m. – 11.00 p.m.	do exercises, have dinner with his family
11.00 p.m. – 2.00 a.m.	write

---

* Others who found inspiration in the horizontal position included Mozart, who composed in bed from 7.00 to 10.00 a.m., Truman Capote (who always wrote lying down, in bed or on a couch – '*as the afternoon wears on, I shift from coffee to mint tea to sherry to martinis*') and Barbara Cartland, who dictated all her novels to a secretary while lying on a sofa with a white fur rug and a hot water bottle.

Lyndon B. Johnson:

6.30 p.m.	wake, read newspapers, start work
2.00 p.m.	exercise (swim or brisk walk)
3.30 p.m.	take nap
4.00 p.m.	start work again, sometimes until 2.00 a.m.

** Churchill said that *'Nature has not intended mankind to work from eight in the morning until midnight without that refreshment of blessed oblivion which, even if it only lasts twenty minutes, is sufficient to renew all the vital forces.'* Naps were so important to him that he even kept a bed at the House of Commons.

The power of the nap

As LBJ shows, just because you've got the most powerful job in the world doesn't mean you can't get a bit of shut-eye in the afternoon. Johnson is said to have learned the habit from his predecessor John F. Kennedy, who, after a mid-morning session of swimming and exercise, would eat lunch in bed, then take a nap. His valet would draw the curtains, his wife Jackie would join him, and then for an hour or two no interruptions at all were allowed. Waking, JFK would take his second bath of the day, then work from 3.30 until 8.00 p.m. Then he'd change for dinner; he wore at least three different sets of clothes every day he was President.

Z

Z

Z

Z

Z

Z

Z

Z

Z   Z   Z

Ronald Reagan's love of sleep became legendary. *'It's true hard work never killed anybody,'* he once said, *'but I figure, why take the chance?'* He frequently napped during the day, but remarked that *'I have left orders to be awakened at any time in case of national emergency, even if I'm in a cabinet meeting.'* Reagan often took Wednesday afternoons off, and left the White House early on Fridays to travel to Camp David, the President's retreat in Maryland. Of his eight years as President, almost one (345 days) was spent in California, much of that time at his ranch near Santa Barbara. *'Show me an executive who works long, hard hours,'* said Reagan, *'and I'll show you a bad executive.'* When it came time to leave office he said that his chair should be inscribed *'Ronald Reagan Slept Here'*.

One time he insisted on getting out of bed, however, was in hospital, recovering from gunshot wounds suffered in the 1981 attempt on his life. Aides entered his room to find him on all fours, wiping up water from the floor. He'd spilled it himself, and was worried that his nurse would get into trouble.

Other famous nappers include . . .

Napoleon – could sleep soundly right before a battle, even with cannon firing near him. His naps made up for his refusal to take a whole night's sleep (or indeed change clothes) for days. When a battle was over, though, he could sleep for 18 hours at a time.

Thomas 'Stonewall' Jackson – the US General was once woken during a battle to be told that fighting was heavy. *'McClellan is only fighting to get away,'* he said. *'In the morning he will be gone.'* Then he went straight back to sleep. Events proved Jackson right. A less dramatic nap was during a church service. *'A man who can go to sleep under Dr Hoge's preaching,'* said someone present, *'can go to sleep anywhere on the face of this earth.'* Jackson's colleague Hunter McGuire said that *'many a night I have kept him on his horse by holding to his coat-tail. He always promised to do as much for me when he had finished his nap. He meant to do it, I am sure, but my turn never came.'*

The hypnagogic state

A very particular form of napping is the 'hypnagogic' state, where you hover between being awake and sleeping. It is said to produce great ideas which can't be accessed in normal consciousness.

Salvador Dali called the state, which he learned from Capuchin monks, his *'slumber with a key'*. In the afternoon he would put a metal pan on the floor, then sit in a chair to doze, holding a heavy metal key between the thumb and forefinger of his left hand. When he fell fully asleep, the key would drop into the pan, waking him up. He claimed this very short nap *'revivified'* his entire *'physical and physic being'*.

Thomas Edison was another great believer in hypnagogia, employing a technique similar to Dali's (he held ball bearings over a metal bowl), though not with the aim of falling fully asleep – if the ball bearings dropped, waking him up, he would start the process all over again. The aim was to hover in the state just *before* full sleep.

Edgar Allan Poe also valued the hypnagogic state, talking of the **'fancies'** he experienced **'only when I am on the brink of sleep, with the consciousness that I am so.'** Others who used similar approaches include Beethoven, Richard Wagner, Walter Scott Albert Einstein and Sir Isaac Newton.

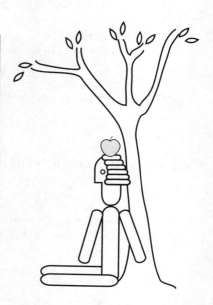

Finally – if sleep eludes you, remember the words of the American writer Philip K. Dick: **'Don't try to solve serious matters in the middle of the night.'**

Food and drink

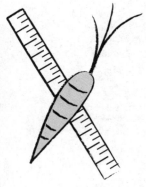

When it comes to food, you can take the simple approach like Franz Kafka – **'So long as you have food in your mouth, you have solved all questions for the time being'** – or Dr John Harvey Kellogg, founder of the cereal company: **'Eat what the monkey eats – simple food and not too much of it.'** Or you can be more particular about it. You don't have to go as far as Howard Hughes, who always measured every carrot he ate – these culinary customs should give you something to chew over:

Breakfast

Alexandre Dumas ate an apple at 7.00 a.m. each day under the Arc de Triomphe.

Abraham Lincoln rarely had anything more than a cup of coffee for breakfast.

Neil Armstrong rarely eats breakfast, a habit picked up during childhood, when he almost always had an early-morning job such as a paper-round. Even during training for Apollo 11 he had no more than a cup of coffee (though on launch day he ate the traditional Apollo astronaut's breakfast of steak and eggs.)

Lunch

Thomas Edison invited prospective research assistants for a bowl of soup. Any who seasoned the soup before tasting it were rejected – he didn't want people who were too ready to make assumptions.

J. Edgar Hoover had the same lunch at the same table every day for 20 years, at Washington's Mayflower Hotel: buttered toast, cottage cheese and grapefruit, salad and chicken soup.

Samuel Johnson: *'Cucumbers should be well sliced and then dressed with pepper and vinegar and then thrown out as good for nothing.'*

Dinner

Orson Welles' usual dinner was two rare steaks and a pint of scotch.

G.K. Chesterton: *'Music with dinner is an insult both to the cook and the violinist.'*

Oil magnate **Nubar Gulbenkian**: *'The best number for a dinner party is two – myself and a damn good head waiter.'*

C.S. Lewis read while he ate. He once said that *'eating and reading are two pleasures that combine admirably. Of course not all books are suitable for mealtime reading. It would be a kind of blasphemy to read poetry at table. What one wants is a gossipy, formless book which can be opened anywhere. The ones I learned so to use at Bookham [a village in Surrey where he studied with a tutor while a young man] were Boswell, and a translation of Herodotus, and Lang's History of English Literature. Tristram Shandy, Elia and the Anatomy of Melancholy are all good for the same purpose.'* He also noted that *'you can never get a cup of tea large enough or a book long enough to suit me.'*

Louis XVIII of France had his cutlets and chops cooked between two thin steaks, to preserve their juices.

When **President Obama's** team gathered on 1 May 2011 to watch a live feed of the raid on Osama Bin Laden's compound in Pakistan, they ordered pizzas from several different takeaway restaurants, to ensure that one big order didn't alert people to something big happening at the White House on a Sunday.

Michael Caine on what he learned from his time owning restaurants: *'The secret, apart from your choice of chef, is having great bread and coffee. The bread's the first thing they taste and the coffee the last.'*

Ronald Reagan's love of jelly beans, and in particular the American brand Jelly Bellies, was so well-known that over 3 tons of the sweets were shipped to Washington to be served during the inauguration festivities when he became President. Red and white ones already existed, but a blue one had to be specially made. Jelly Bellies were served in the Oval Office during his tenure (the black ones were his favourite), and also on Air Force One, where a special holder had to be designed so they wouldn't spill during turbulent flights. Reagan even sent some on a 1983 Space Shuttle mission as a surprise for the astronauts.

Looking after your guests

Lewis Carroll kept a record of every meal given to his guests so as not to serve them the same thing twice.

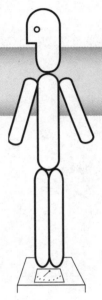

Edward VII weighed visitors before they left Sandringham to ensure they'd been well-fed.

Margaret Thatcher was more concerned about waiting staff than her guests. When a Chequers waitress spilled soup into someone's lap, Thatcher leapt up with concern – not for the guest but for the tearful waitress. Another who dropped a tray of canapés on the Downing Street carpet was told: 'Don't worry, dear – pick them up and give them to Carol.' (Thatcher's choice of food when not entertaining was very simple; a favourite dish to cook herself in the Number Ten kitchen was coronation chicken. On the night of her election victory in 1979 she ordered a Chinese takeaway.)

Drink

Henry Ford always drank warm water, to avoid his body having to waste energy by heating it up. He maintained his fitness – he could do handstands at the age of seventy-five, and in his late fifties could jump in the air and kick a cigar off a fireplace.

If there are three cans of Coke in David Beckham's fridge he will throw one away to achieve symmetry.

Honoré de Balzac drank ten or more espresso coffees a day, while Beethoven made each cup of coffee using exactly sixty beans. Steven Spielberg, on the other hand, tried coffee as a child, hated the taste and has never drunk it since.

The broadcaster **Ned Sherrin** found the teabags in the BBC canteen very weak – so to avoid waiting would use two per cup.

'*A mathematician,*' said Paul Erdos, '*is a machine for turning coffee into theorems.*' He should know – for the last twenty-five years of his life he worked for nineteen hours a day on maths, drinking coffee to stay awake. (He was also helped each day by 10 to 20 milligrams of Benzedrine or Ritalin.)

The demon drink

Coleridge drank ale in the middle of the morning.

At the age of sixty-eight, during a speech lasting three-and-a-quarter hours, Disraeli drank two bottles of brandy.

Ray Charles drank half a mug of black coffee and Bols gin (with two sugars) every day after he gave up heroin.

Before filming the camel scenes in *Lawrence of Arabia* (and unknown to director David Lean), **Peter O'Toole** and **Omar Sharif** would drink brandy and milk cocktails to steady their nerves.

Harold Wilson always carried a supply of Lucozade on tour, as he liked to sip it while giving speeches. He also took his own blue glasses to drink it from, as he worried that in a clear glass the Lucozade would look like scotch.

The opposite of this was **Dean Martin**. He knew that people liked to think of him as a boozer. He certainly wasn't teetotal, but neither did he drink as much as people thought he did – so on stage he drank apple juice, knowing that people would think it was whisky.

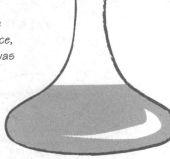

And finally . . .

To tie together the two themes of this chapter – food and sleep – we turn to the artist Henry Fuseli. He ate raw pork chops before going to bed so that he would dream vividly. It worked, and his dreams inspired him to paint his most famous work 'The Nightmare'. The novelist Patrick McGrath heard this story, and copied the method: *'I've often eaten cheese late at night so that I'll dream vividly. I rather enjoy it. Cheese does have certain properties that act upon the neuro-physiological system to stimulate dreaming.'*

The eighteenth-century German poet Johann Schiller kept rotten apples in his desk. The revolting smell, he said, inspired creativity.

'**GOOD DAY AT THE OFFICE, DARLING?**'

The work environment

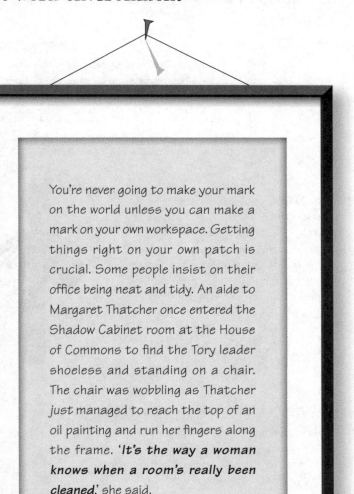

You're never going to make your mark on the world unless you can make a mark on your own workspace. Getting things right on your own patch is crucial. Some people insist on their office being neat and tidy. An aide to Margaret Thatcher once entered the Shadow Cabinet room at the House of Commons to find the Tory leader shoeless and standing on a chair. The chair was wobbling as Thatcher just managed to reach the top of an oil painting and run her fingers along the frame. **'It's the way a woman knows when a room's really been cleaned,'** she said.

Dark days (and nights)

Warren Buffett keeps the blinds in his office closed so that he can't look out of the window and be distracted by the view.

Elvis Presley tended to record his songs through the night. For 'Are You Lonesome Tonight?' (recorded at 3.00 a.m.), he insisted on virtual darkness in the studio to ensure the right mood. Listen closely at the end and you can hear him bump into a microphone stand.

American writer **Nicholson Baker** gets up at 4.00 a.m. and works in the dark – he even has the computer screen turned off, so he cannot actually see what he is typing. At 6.00 a.m. he then goes back to bed, resurfacing at 8.00 a.m. to edit his earlier work.

Coming into the light a little, **Honoré de Balzac** worked at a table lit by four candles.* He would often work for 15 hours or more at a stretch; he claimed to have once worked for 48 hours with only 3 hours of rest in the middle.

At the other end of the (light) spectrum is the German writer Gunter Grass, who needs daylight to work effectively. When he writes at night, he says, the words come easily, but when he reads them back in the morning they're no good.

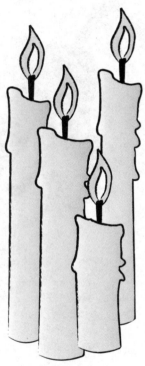

* This was the same number of candles that preceded the choir into Westminster Abbey at Ronnie Barker's memorial service in 2006, a reference to his most famous sketch. Barker used to say the sketch was the only time (out of thousands) that he took up a viewer's idea. A hardware shop owner in Hayes wrote describing a real incident, suggesting it as the basis for comedy.

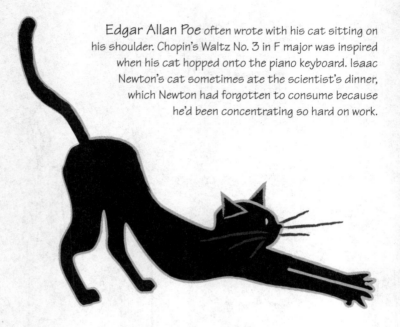

Edgar Allan Poe often wrote with his cat sitting on his shoulder. Chopin's Waltz No. 3 in F major was inspired when his cat hopped onto the piano keyboard. Isaac Newton's cat sometimes ate the scientist's dinner, which Newton had forgotten to consume because he'd been concentrating so hard on work.

Michael Bukht (who as Michael Barry was famous as a TV chef) worked as an executive at the radio station Classic FM. He didn't like the company's open-plan offices, so whenever he wanted privacy he would lean back in his chair with eyes closed and a yellow Post-It note on his forehead saying 'Don't interrupt — I'm thinking'.

The comedy writer Jonathan Lynn: *'Comedy in my opinion is all about human weakness. I keep a copy of the seven deadly sins on my desk: lust, avarice, greed, envy and so on. These are the staples of comedy.'*

Robert Maxwell had five telephones on his desk, three of which were unconnected, used for fake conversations with world leaders to impress visitors. Similarly a young Richard Branson used to get people to go out to phoneboxes and ring him during meetings so that he would appear in demand.

Mussolini used the Papal suite in Rome's Palazzo Venezia as his office, just so that visitors would have to walk an intimidating 60ft across the empty marble floor to reach his desk. This trick was copied by Harry Cohn, the founder of Columbia Pictures (who had a picture of Il Duce on his wall). Cohn was an intimidating person in general. He once sacked an employee who had stood up for him, explaining that *'every time I see you from now on I'll know that I owe you a favour, and I cannot have that.'* If he did help anyone or give money to a charity he would say *'Don't tell anybody I did this – I don't want to lose my reputation.'*

Another office trick employed by **Cohn** was giving his visitor a lower chair. His fellow Hollywood mogul Louis B. Mayer went one better – he had a platform subtly designed into the floor on his side of the desk.

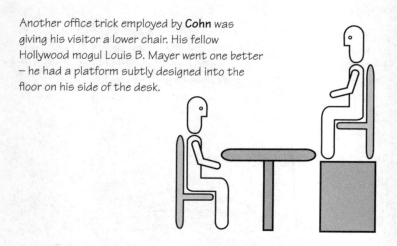

For some people a desk simply isn't big enough: the writer Edward de Bono's flat is filled with piles of papers, on top of each one a white tile bearing a number, according to the pile's importance.

Each morning the writer John Cheever would put on his suit (he only had one), then take the lift from his Manhattan apartment down to a room in the building's basement, where he would strip down to his boxer shorts and work until lunchtime. Then he would get dressed again, go back upstairs for lunch, then repeat the routine in the afternoon.

The political biographer Robert Caro (acclaimed for his lifelong work on Lyndon B. Johnson) wears a jacket and tie to his New York office to remind himself that his work is just that – work. He and his wife Ina, who is also a Johnson scholar, have an agreement not to talk about work at home, to the extent that they exclude books from their dining and living rooms.

Georges Auguste Escoffier, the legendary Ritz chef in the late nineteenth and early twentieth centuries, wore shoes with raised heels to let him see the pans at the back of the ranges.

The cinema and theatre director **Ingmar Bergman** was famous for demanding quiet. Rehearsing a play in 1996, he stood outside the hall half an hour before the start each day to make sure the actors weren't socialising with each other.

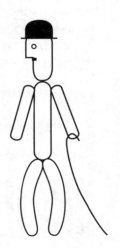

Charlie Chaplin never used scripts. He would start from a basic premise (e.g. 'Charlie enters a health spa'), and after having sets constructed would improvise around them. The perfectionist director would do multiple takes (sometimes more than a hundred), and was very demanding on his actors and crew. The film's story would emerge as Chaplin went along, often meaning that earlier scenes had to be re-shot (at great expense) to fit in.

Jim Morrison recorded the vocals to The Doors' 'L.A. Woman' in the recording studio's bathroom because he wanted a fuller sound. Legendary British producer Joe Meek turned his house on London's Holloway Road into his studio. String sections were recorded in the hallway, backing vocalists in the bathroom, while brass players had to stand on the stairs.

Doing it by the book

David Blunkett listens to the audio tapes on which he 'reads' his documents at double the normal speed (other people find them incomprehensible like this).

Oscar Wilde was a skilled speed-reader. *'When I was a boy at school, I was looked upon as a prodigy by my associates because, quite frequently, I would, for a wager, read a three-volume novel in half an hour so closely as to be able to give an accurate résumé of the plot of the story; by one hour's reading I was enabled to give a fair narrative of the incidental scenes and the most pertinent dialogue.'*

Gary Rhodes has about 2,500 cookery books.

Sarah Palin's autocue during the 2008 US Presidential campaign spelled the word 'nuclear' as 'new-clear' to remind her how to say it.

Being contacted

Bill Murray no longer has an agent. To contact him you leave a message on a freephone number. He checks these (sometimes infrequently), and calls back if he's interested. One person was asked to leave a number on which Murray himself could leave a message, so he could reply without talking to her. He occasionally asks for scripts to be left in a phone booth near his home in upstate New York.

> Queen Victoria was equally picky about being disturbed. She didn't allow people to knock on doors — they had to scratch them instead.

Richard Branson: *'I still far prefer talking to people to having e-mail. I don't do my own BlackBerry. I can dictate my e-mails.'*

> Shirley MacLaine: *'I don't do email. I refuse. I want to hear the tenor of the voice and the spaces in between the words of the person I'm talking to.'*

Alastair Campbell took the same approach while working for Tony Blair at 10 Downing Street: *'I never used a computer other than to write — I used it as a word processor. I never sent e-mails or used the internet.'* Aides would read and reply to emails on his behalf.

Riders cause a storm

Lists of stars' demands about their working arrangements (their 'riders') can be . . . well, demanding:

> Filming *Cat on a Hot Tin Roof* for British television, **Robert Wagner** and Natalie Wood specified a minimum size for their dressing room. A lawyer found that the room was narrower than stipulated – so builders were called in to rectify the matter.

Frank Sinatra's representatives would measure the gap between tacks holding down the red carpet from his dressing room to the stage – a maximum of 18 inches was allowed.

Luciano Pavarotti had to be met at airports with a BMW 8 series – he could fit into a 7 series, but couldn't get out of it without struggling in an undignified manner. He also refused to be interviewed on television without a table to sit behind.

One of the most notorious riders was the rock band **Van Halen**'s insistence on a bowl of M&Ms backstage – with all the brown ones removed. But the band's singer David Lee Roth explained that this wasn't because they were prima donnas – it was simply to test whether the promoter had read the contract (which covered other more important technical and safety issues).

How to get the best out of those who work for you

The inexperienced actor who provided the voice for Mission Control in *2001: A Space Odyssey* kept nervously tapping his feet as the lines were recorded. Instead of losing his temper, director **Stanley Kubrick** folded up a towel, put it beneath the actor's feet and told him to tap away as much as he liked.

To get a more violent reaction from **Richard E. Grant** in the *Withnail and I* scene that has him swigging from a can of lighter fluid, director Bruce Robinson filled the can – which in rehearsals had contained water – with vinegar. As the teetotal Grant was playing an alcoholic, Robinson had already made him drink a bottle of champagne and half a bottle of vodka one night to know what it was like to be drunk.

A cameraman who worked for Lord Snowdon: *'There was never any Us and Them. If he was asked to stay to a meal by a client, he wouldn't sit down at the table unless I was included too. Once, when we were photographing Field Marshal Lord Montgomery's grandchildren, Monty said to Tony, "Oh, you'll stay for a spot of lunch? Your man can get a bite at the pub up the road." And Tony said at once, "No, I'm terribly sorry, we've got to go back to London." He simply wasn't going to have it.'*

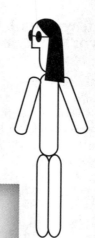

Ozzy Osbourne on his personal assistant Tony Dennis: *'I think the main reason we get along so well is his Geordie accent. It means I haven't got a clue what he's on about half the time – and he says the same thing about me.'*

In 1914 Henry Ford introduced a minimum wage of $5 per day, more than double his previous rate – it instantly ended his staff turnover problems.

Napoleon Bonaparte: *'The art of war is to dispose one's troops so that they are everywhere at the same time.'*

Steve Jobs, head of Apple, had a habit of dropping in on his employees unannounced, just to see what they were working on. *'You might go a while without seeing him,'* said one of them at the time, *'but you are constantly aware of his presence. You are constantly aware that what you're doing will either please or displease him.'*

Walter Raleigh: *'The employer generally gets the employees he deserves.'*

Sometimes your workers can be unpaid ones. The author Anthony Horowitz makes his two sons read all his Alex Rider novels. *'They've had a tremendous input right from the beginning . . . One of the main things they did early on was stop me using phrases or terms that were dated. They'd leave me notes on the manuscript. And the worst you can get is "Dad, that's a bit cringe". You feel like the washed-up magician in the corner at a kids' party.'*

Enemy exchanges

Sometimes your workplace comfort depends on knowing that your opponent is uncomfortable. The English cricketer **Geoff Boycott**, for instance, deliberately wound the other side's bowlers up by singing 'I've got you under my skin'.

Similarly the British Embassy in Moscow found a cunning way of annoying Stalin. Their building was directly opposite the Soviet leader's bedroom in the Kremlin, meaning that his sworn capitalist enemy was the first thing Stalin had to see on waking up every morning. Immensely irritated by this, he ordered that they be offered another building – any other building in the city they wanted. Knowing exactly why the offer had been made, the British politely declined, saying they'd much rather stay where they were.

The write stuff

Words per day

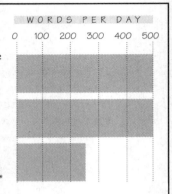

Ernest Hemingway – 500 – exactly – he would stop at word 501 no matter how inspired he was.

Joanna Trollope – 500

Anthony Trollope – 250 words per quarter of an hour between 5.30 and 8.30 a.m., with his watch in front of him*

WORDS PER DAY
0   100   200   300   400   500

** If he finished a novel before 8.30, he instantly started on the next one. For a long time Trollope combined his writing with a day job at the Royal Mail. Also he hunted at least twice a week. Nevertheless his regime let him produce forty-nine novels in thirty-five years, and he advised would-be writers to follow his example: **'Let their work be to them as is his common work to the common labourer. No gigantic efforts will then be necessary. He need tie no wet towels round his brow, nor sit for thirty hours at his desk without moving – as men have sat, or said that they have sat.'***

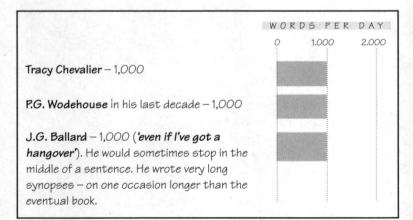

WORDS PER DAY
0   1.000   2.000

Tracy Chevalier – 1,000

P.G. Wodehouse in his last decade – 1,000

J.G. Ballard – 1,000 (**'even if I've got a hangover'**). He would sometimes stop in the middle of a sentence. He wrote very long synopses – on one occasion longer than the eventual book.

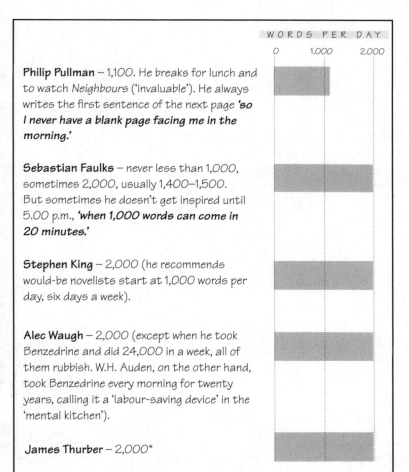

WORDS PER DAY

0   1.000   2.000

Philip Pullman – 1,100. He breaks for lunch and to watch *Neighbours* ('invaluable'). He always writes the first sentence of the next page *'so I never have a blank page facing me in the morning.'*

Sebastian Faulks – never less than 1,000, sometimes 2,000, usually 1,400–1,500. But sometimes he doesn't get inspired until 5.00 p.m., *'when 1,000 words can come in 20 minutes.'*

Stephen King – 2,000 (he recommends would-be novelists start at 1,000 words per day, six days a week).

Alec Waugh – 2,000 (except when he took Benzedrine and did 24,000 in a week, all of them rubbish. W.H. Auden, on the other hand, took Benzedrine every morning for twenty years, calling it a 'labour-saving device' in the 'mental kitchen').

James Thurber – 2,000*

* *'I never quite know when I'm not writing. Sometimes my wife comes up to me at a party and says, "Dammit, Thurber, stop writing." She usually catches me in the middle of a paragraph. I have to do it that way on account of my eyes. [Thurber had bad eyesight.] I still write occasionally – in the proper sense of the word – using black crayon on yellow paper and getting perhaps twenty words to the page. My usual method, though, is to spend the mornings turning over the text in my mind. Then in the afternoon, between two and five, I call in a secretary and dictate to her.'*

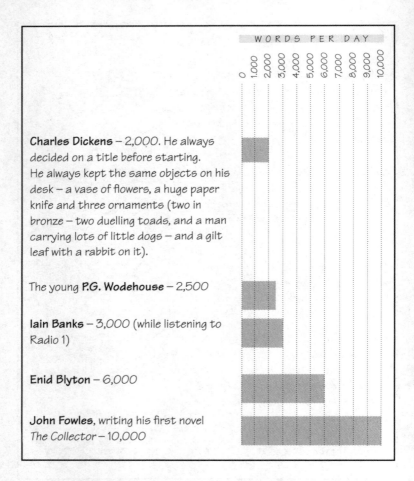

WORDS PER DAY

0 · 1,000 · 2,000 · 3,000 · 4,000 · 5,000 · 6,000 · 7,000 · 8,000 · 9,000 · 10,000

Charles Dickens – 2,000. He always decided on a title before starting. He always kept the same objects on his desk – a vase of flowers, a huge paper knife and three ornaments (two in bronze – two duelling toads, and a man carrying lots of little dogs – and a gilt leaf with a rabbit on it).

The young **P.G. Wodehouse** – 2,500

Iain Banks – 3,000 (while listening to Radio 1)

Enid Blyton – 6,000

John Fowles, writing his first novel *The Collector* – 10,000

Of course you can take the 'quick' approach to getting your words done. The newspaper magnate **William Randolph Hearst** sent the renowned astronomer Percival Lowell a telegram saying: **'Is there life on Mars? Please cable one thousand words.'** Lowell responded with **'Nobody knows'** repeated 500 times.

How writers write

Dan Brown keeps an hourglass on his desk; every time it runs out he breaks to perform press-ups and sit-ups.

Michael Ondaatje writes everything longhand and then literally cuts and pastes, with scissors and tape.

John Irving always writes the last sentence of a novel first. Lewis Carroll did the same with *The Hunting of the Snark.*

Kingsley Amis kept not only the manuscript of the preliminary notes for *Lucky Jim*, but also the pencils and pens with which he'd written it.

John Steinbeck used 300 pencils to write *East of Eden.* Every day he would sharpen them, then warm up by writing a letter to his friend and publisher Pascal Covici. These letters were written on the left-hand page of a notebook Covici had given him. After doing this, Steinbeck would write that day's section of the novel on the right-hand page (about 1,500 words).

Somerset Maugham would read Voltaire's *Candide* before starting work. Willa Cather read the Bible.

Vladimir Nabokov used 5in x 8in index cards to compose the scenes in his novels. Once he'd got the chapters in the right order he would write the book out in full.

For all his reputation as a technological innovator, film director George Lucas writes everything in longhand in a loose-leaf binder.

As P.G. Wodehouse finished each page, he would pin it to his office wall at a height indicating how good it was. Pages still needing work were lower down; the aim was to get the whole manuscript up to the picture rail.

When Jane Austen began writing she used very small pieces of paper, easily hideable under a blotter in case anyone came in.

Anton Chekhov wrote in a chalet on his estate, raising a flag when he was ready to receive visitors.

Don DeLillo uses a manual typewriter:
'When I was working on The Names I devised
a new method - new to me, anyway. When I
finished a paragraph, even a three-line
paragraph, I automatically went to a fresh
page to start the new paragraph. No crowded
pages. This enabled me to see a given set of
sentences more clearly. It made rewriting
easier and more effective. The white space
on the page helped me concentrate more
deeply on what I'd written.'

Umberto Eco writes in a converted church.
On one floor he writes on a computer, on another
uses a typewriter, on the third in longhand.

Roald Dahl had a brick writing hut specially built in his
Buckinghamshire garden. It contained his favourite wing-
backed armchair, as well as treasured possessions like his
own hip bone and a huge ball made from foil sweet wrappers.
He wrote on lined yellow legal pads shipped over from
America, supported on a wooden board stretched across his
lap. 'When I'm in this place,' he said, 'it's lovely. It's my nest,
my womb.' To discourage his children from disturbing him he
used to tell them there were wolves in there.

Henrik Ibsen had a portrait of his enemy August Stringberg facing his desk. 'I cannot write a line,' he said, 'without that madman standing and staring down at me with his mad eyes.' He wanted Strindberg to 'hang there and watch' while he wrote. Similarly the BBC Director-General Hugh Carleton Greene bought a painting depicting his arch-enemy Mary Whitehouse with five breasts. He said he wanted it for his office so he could have something to throw darts at.

Will Self: 'First drafts as early in the morning as possible, then second, then third (retyping, I work on a manual). Once the first draft is 80 per cent completed I start on the second, so that there's a conveyor belt of drafts in progress: this helps me to grasp the totality of the book.'

Frank Skinner writes everything (sitcoms, sketches, his autobiography) on computer, but his stand-up is still written freehand. 'Perhaps it's simply that I was writing stand-up before I owned or knew how to operate a computer, and old habits die hard.' Skinner keeps a model of Wile E. Coyote from the Road Runner cartoons on his desk. 'He's the one who gets blown up, fried, crushed and generally badly hurt in his pursuit of the Road Runner, but keeps going. He's the ultimate symbol of endurance, determination and single-mindedness. When I'm writing a book, a TV show, or stand-up, he looks over me. Fuck failure, keep going.'

> To prepare for writing his *Daily Telegraph* articles (when he was the paper's Brussels correspondent), Boris Johnson would rant. According to his colleague Sonia Purnell: 'Like Superman, he would undergo a startling and virtually instantaneous transformation from Bumbling Boris to Bilious Boris before penning yet another explosive tract.'
>
> Elizabeth I always wrote with a swan's quill, despite the fact that most people found a goose quill easier to use. A swan quill lasted fifty times longer.

They wrote standing up

Winston Churchill

Virginia Woolf – (to ape her artist sister, whose work she felt was taken more seriously)

Ernest Hemingway – (despite the fact he said the first rule for writers was **'apply the seat of the pants to the seat of a chair'**).

Tom Wolfe

Philip Roth

Lord Palmerston used to work standing up at a desk so that if he fell asleep he would land on the desk and be able to carry on working. (He always put in a very long working day.)

Vladimir Nabokov – **'After waking up between six and seven in the morning, I write till ten-thirty, generally at a lectern which faces a bright corner of the room instead of the bright audiences of my professorial days.'** At 8.30 a.m. he broke for breakfast, over which he also read his mail. **'One kind of letter that goes into the wastepaper basket at once, with its enclosed stamped envelope and my picture, is the one from the person who tells me he has a large collection of autographs and would like to add my name, which he misspells.'**

So you want to be a writer?

Somerset Maugham: *'There are three rules for writing a novel. Unfortunately, no one knows what they are.'*

John Updike: *'Fiction is a little like handwriting. It comes out to be you no matter what you do.'*

Elmore Leonard was asked how he managed to keep his books' plots moving along so well. He replied: *'I leave out the parts that people skip.'*

Dorothy Parker: *'My subjective experience [of writing] is that each day is some fresh hell.'*

The American writer T.H. White: *'Write your own name a hundred times and you will be bored; seven hundred times and you will be exasperated; seven thousand times, and your brains will be reeling in your head. Then you realise that you have only written one-tenth of a new novel, and you will be lucky to escape the madhouse. And yet you haven't experienced the full of it. Your own name can at least be written down mechanically. You need have no ideas. You can work like a sweated labourer doing piece-work in a factory. But the novelist has to write down different names, nouns, verbs, prepositions, adjectives, reeling across the page. They have to make sense.'*

E.L. Doctorow: *'Writing a novel is like driving a car at night. You can only see as far as your headlights, but you can make the whole trip that way.'*

The comedian Steve Martin once wrote a novel: *'I think I did pretty well, considering I started out with nothing but a bunch of blank paper.'*

THE BODY BEAUTIFUL

'There is only one thing people like that is good for them,' the American journalist Edgar Watson Howe once said. 'A good night's sleep.' This is probably an unnecessarily cynical view. There are all sorts of things that people do to keep themselves in shape, some of them really not that taxing. Just as there are all sorts of shortcuts that they take to improve their appearance. The human body is an incredible thing – so come on, let's get physical . . .

Walking

Miles per day

Michael Caine – 4	
Thomas de Quincey – 14 (even at the age of seventy)	
Charles Dickens – 15	
Gladstone – 33 miles in one day while in his sixties	

The American writer Henry David Thoreau: *'Methinks that the moment my legs begin to move, my thoughts begin to flow.'* He expanded on this by saying *'I cannot preserve my health and spirits unless I spend four hours a day at least – and it is commonly more than that – sauntering through the woods and over the hills and fields absolutely free from all worldly engagements . . .'*

In 1846 **Charles Darwin** constructed what he called a 'sandwalk' near his home, Down House in Kent, a circular sand-covered path he referred to as his 'thinking path'. He would put a number of pieces of flint at the start of the walk, then flick one away with his stick each time he passed them. When all the pieces were gone he knew he'd completed the required number of laps.

Mozart said many of his best musical ideas came to him while he was out walking.

C.S. Lewis always took a walk after lunch: *'Not, except at rare intervals, with a friend. Walking and talking are two very great pleasures, but it is a mistake to combine them. Our own noise blots out the sounds and silences of the outdoor world; and talking leads almost inevitably to smoking, and then farewell to nature as far as one of our senses is concerned. The only friend to walk with is one (such as I found, during the holidays, in Arthur) who so exactly shares your taste for each mood of the countryside that a glance, a halt, or at most a nudge, is enough to assure us that the pleasure is shared.'*

Alternative activities . . .

If walking is a touch boring for you, you might like to follow Eric Idle's advice: *'As a writer, I swim. That's what keeps my shoulders from aching all day.'* Less conventional use of the pool was made a young Frank Sinatra, who was forced by his mother to practise underwater swimming as a way of developing his ability to hold long breaths.

The famous mathematician G.H. Hardy never worked more than four hours a day, reserving the afternoon for cricket and tennis. His best ideas, he said, came when he wasn't *'doing work'.*

If anyone tells you that you shouldn't drink while you're trying to get fit, refer them to the story of British boxing legend Henry Cooper. He was very light for a heavyweight, and needed to put weight on in the run-up to his fight with Muhammad Ali. So his trainer made him drink half a pint of draught Guinness with a double vintage port every lunchtime.

If you want to get really wacky you can follow the lead of William Beveridge (the British politician who founded the post-war welfare state) – he had an ice-cold bath every morning at 6 o'clock. Or you could copy the French clergyman and politician Cardinal Richelieu, who exercised every day by jumping over furniture.

Then again, there's one other thing you can try. As H.G. Wells said: *'To make love periodically, with some grace and pride and freshness, seems to be, for most of us, a necessary condition to efficient working.'*

Caring by not caring

Socrates never washed or wore shoes.

Ralph Richardson started smoking at the age of eighty – he said by then it was too late for it to make any difference.

The American economist Beardsley Ruml: *'If you ever hear of me dropping dead on a tennis court, you'll know I was crossing it to get a Scotch and soda.'*

The American golfer Phil Mickelson is actually right-handed – he only plays left-handed because as a toddler he used to stand opposite his dad and mirror his swing. By the time his parents realised he was right-handed he was doing so well that they decided not to change anything.

The theatre director Joan Littlewood gave the young Richard Harris his first break in acting. In rehearsal she once made him take all his clothes off. *'Now make me believe you are fully dressed,'* she said *'Until you're prepared to expose yourself, you'll never be any good as an actor.'*

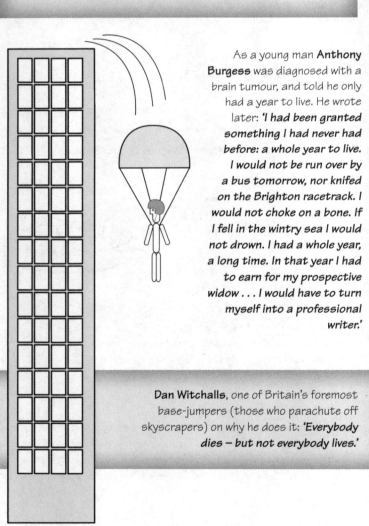

As a young man **Anthony Burgess** was diagnosed with a brain tumour, and told he only had a year to live. He wrote later: *'I had been granted something I had never had before: a whole year to live. I would not be run over by a bus tomorrow, nor knifed on the Brighton racetrack. I would not choke on a bone. If I fell in the wintry sea I would not drown. I had a whole year, a long time. In that year I had to earn for my prospective widow . . . I would have to turn myself into a professional writer.'*

Dan Witchalls, one of Britain's foremost base-jumpers (those who parachute off skyscrapers) on why he does it: *'Everybody dies – but not everybody lives.'*

Moving for money

Some tips from the professionals . . .

BANG!

Jesse Owens: *'I let my feet spend as little time on the ground as possible. From the air, fast down, and from the ground, fast up.'*

After his Olympic success Owens made personal appearances where he would race and beat horses. His trick was that he always raced high-strung thoroughbreds, knowing the starting gun would frighten them and make them jump.

After a marathon, Paula Radcliffe takes two weeks off. *'The first week I'm all right, I'm having a lie-in in the morning, doing different things and recovering from the race.'* But then things change. *'You suddenly realise that running is your stress release. In the second week I'm dying to go for a run.'* Radcliffe is well-known for trying new things, be they ice baths or emu oil. She even started wearing a mouth guard on her bottom jaw to correct an imbalance in her lower spine.

Radcliffe's solution to pain during a race? *'Use dissociation techniques to take your mind off the pain. Slowly count to 100 three times.'* At Radcliffe's pace, this takes a mile.

The organisers of the New York marathon want the winners to look their best, so have towels at the finish line to wipe saliva from the runners' faces. They even airbrush it from photos that are to be used for publicity purposes.

The body – a user's guide

Ronnie Wood on having his teeth whitened: *'I said I want the veneer to be white and they said, "Oh, it's not Ronnie Wood to have bloody Hollywood teeth. So we got a built-in stain."'*

Reggie Kray became known for his 'cigarette punch'. Offering his victim a cigarette with one hand, he would quickly punch them with the other. Their mouth would be open in readiness for the cigarette, meaning that the jaw would break more easily.

The philosopher **Michel de Montaigne** said he was grateful he'd suffered from kidney stones, because they allowed him to know what it was to be free of pain.

David Cameron likes to make his speeches with a full bladder, so deliberately refrains from using the toilet in advance of one. He learned this technique from Enoch Powell, who said: *'You should do nothing to decrease the tension before making a big speech. If anything you should seek to increase it.'*

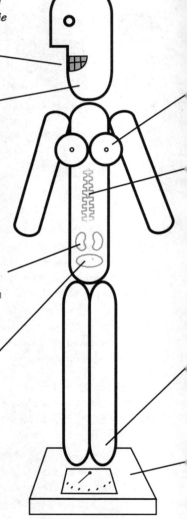

Shirley MacLaine used to put 2.5mm pearls in her bra so people would think they were her nipples.

To stop his spine from curving, which would mean he'd lose height, **Cliff Richard** stands up to watch TV.

Jonathan Lynn (the co-writer of *Yes Minister*) says that audiences won't laugh if they can't see the character's feet (for instance if the character is standing behind a sofa). He has no idea why, but has found it to be true. Buster Keaton said the same thing, and indeed stopped making films when they brought in widescreen because it meant his feet wouldn't be visible. *'How will they laugh if they can't see my feet?'* he asked.

The American children's TV presenter **Fred Rogers** always kept his weight at 143lbs. Having seen one day that this is how heavy he was, he realised it matched the number of letters in 'I love you'.

MONEY, MONEY, MONEY

It's vulgar to talk about money, so we'll keep this short —
but there are a few lessons about the folding stuff worth
learning . . .

Oscar Wilde: *'It is better to have a permanent income
than to be fascinating.'*

Karl Marx's mother: *'I wish you would make some
capital instead of just writing about it.'*

Bernie Ecclestone:
*'First get on, then get rich,
then get honest.'*

H.L. Mencken:
*'If someone says "this isn't
about money", it's about
money.'*

Isaac Newton kept a box of guineas on his windowsill to test the honesty of those who worked for him.

Rembrandt's students, knowing how much the artist loved money, would paint coins on the floor to entice him to pick them up. Rembrandt's painting 'The Night Watch' was commissioned by a group of eighteen merchants who acted as part-time civic guards. Rembrandt told each of the eighteen that the more he paid, the more prominently he would be featured in the final painting.

As a young musician on the road Ray Charles insisted on being paid in single dollar bills. This made it impossible for unscrupulous promoters to take advantage of his blindness.

Look after the pennies . . .

The American industrialist John D. Rockefeller, on a tour of one of his factories, noted that forty drops of solder were being used to seal kerosene cans. He asked the foreman to try using thirty-eight drops. Some of the cans leaked. They raised it to thirty-nine drops – and none of the cans leaked. *'That one drop of solder,'* recalled Rockefeller, *'saved $2,500 the first year: but the export business kept on increasing after that and doubled, quadrupled, became immensely greater than it was then – and the saving has gone steadily along, one drop on each can, and has amounted since to many hundreds of thousands of dollars.'*

Ernest Hemingway said that his wife's swimming pool had cost him his *'last penny'*. To mark the fact he pushed a one-cent piece into the still-wet cement. It's there to this day – but has turned bright green.

Funny money

John Cleese: 'We [the Monty Python team] didn't start making any real money until The Holy Grail became a success in America. Up till that time, we were earning astonishingly little. I remember a friend of mine called Tony Hendra [who later achieved fame playing Spinal Tap's hapless manager Ian Faith] visiting me in London and watching one of the first series of Monty Python, and laughing a great deal. Afterwards, when we started talking about what we were paid for it, I told him I was getting £240 a show, and he laughed even more than he'd done at the show. He fell off the sofa. It was one of the few times I've seen someone literally do that. By American standards that was hilariously small.'

His co-Python **Eric Idle** on the same subject: **'The difference between English and American humour is $150 a minute.'**

The rich . . .

The American railroad enterpreneur Cornelius Vanderbilt never owned a chequebook, writing his cheques instead on blank writing paper.

W.C. Fields got free drinks by always using a cheque to pay for a drink, knowing that the bar owner would frame rather than cash it.

MONEY, MONEY, MONEY

One way of showing off your wealth is by not showing it off. The New York headquarters of JP Morgan at 23 Wall Street were designed to achieve this in two ways. Firstly the firm's name didn't appear on the building, as they were aware that everyone knew who they were anyway. And it was deliberately constructed with only four storeys. Most companies had to maximise their return from a plot by building as high as possible, a trend which fuelled the 1920s skyscraper boom. But Morgan showed that their riches put them beyond such concerns.

When asked what his hit 'American Pie' meant, Don McLean replied *'it means I never have to work again.'*

The immensely rich Nubar Gulbenkian was a fan of London taxis, saying that they could *'turn on a sixpence – whatever that is.'* Asked by a form for his position in life he wrote *'enviable'*.

Andrew Loog-Oldham, first manager of the Rolling Stones: *'When you have someone to press the up button of the hotel elevator for you, it's generally all over.'*

Sometimes it's not how much, it's how you earn it that counts – even to the rich. When Sting began to doubt himself, he went out to a Tube station in London and busked. He made £40, a sum that reassured him he could still please an audience. He pulled a hat down over his eyes to disguise himself. One woman recognised him, but the man behind her talked her out of it: *'You silly cow. It's not him. He's a multi-millionaire.'*

. . . and the poor

Some words of comfort for when the bank balance is making you unbalanced:

Herbert Hoover: *'About the time we think we can make ends meet, somebody moves the ends.'*

Mary Quant: *'Having money is rather like being a blonde. It is more fun but not vital.'*

Robert Graves: *'There's no money in poetry, but then there's no poetry in money, either.'*

Thomas Jefferson: *'The glow of one warm thought is to me worth more than money.'*

And on the subject of losing it . . .

Lord Amherst: *'There are three ways of losing money: racing is the quickest, women the most pleasant, and farming the most certain.'*

Finding funds

Richard Branson, asked what is the quickest way to become a millionaire: *'Borrow fivers off everyone.'*

Anthony Burgess: *'I refuse no reasonable offer of work and very few unreasonable ones.'*

When you're negotiating about money, you might – or might not – care to follow the example of **Boris Johnson,** who as Mayor of London was dealing with Prime Minister David Cameron about the capital's budget. At one point Johnson leapt over the table and tried to wrestle Cameron's briefing notes from him.

If you've chosen a job that you love but which pays badly, and ever start to regret the decision, remember the words of J.M. Barrie: *'Nothing is really work unless you would rather be doing something else.'*

AND RELAX . . .
HOW TO SPEND
YOUR DOWNTIME

A successful life contains more than just work — you need to consider how you spend your time off. Your time out. Your 'you time' time. If you don't chill correctly, you'll pay the price when you're back at the desk/in the laboratory/ up the mountain. At home and on your hols, relaxation is the name of the game — here's how some of the great and good have managed it.

King Otto, ruler of Bavaria from 1886 to 1913, shot a peasant every morning to start his day. Or at least he thought he did. Actually one of his advisers would hand him a rifle loaded with blank bullets, while another would dress as a peasant, pretending to fall and die when he'd been 'shot'.

Winston Churchill relaxed by painting, completing 500 canvases during his life. The hobby helped counter his famous 'black dog' depressions: *'I know nothing which, without exhausting the body, more entirely absorbs the mind. Whatever the worries of the hour, once the picture has begun to flow along there is no room for them in the mental screen. They pass out into shadow and darkness . . . When I get to heaven I mean to spend a considerable portion of my first million years in painting, and so get to the bottom of the subject.'*

Gladstone read 22,000 books in his lifetime. US President John Quincy Adams read the Bible in its entirety every year.

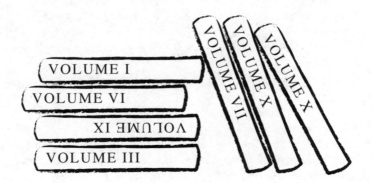

Kenneth Williams learned four new words every day.

Instead of using proper tobacco in his pipe, **P.G. Wodehouse** crumbled up cigars sent to him by his publisher.

Walt Disney smoked up to 70 cigarettes a day. He preferred them unfiltered – his daughter bought him ones with filters, which he would snap off whenever she wasn't present.

Party animals

The BBC news presenter **Emily Maitlis** always uses the same trick for getting rid of bores at a party – she carries two drinks, allowing her to claim that she's taking one of them to someone else. Michael Caine tackles the same problem by muttering to his wife Shakira 'lose the fridge' (Cockney rhyming slang: 'fridge freezer' – 'geezer'). This is her cue to claim that they have to be moving on.

The American writer Nora Ephron also used her spouse at parties: if she pinched her husband's arm as someone approached it was a sign for 'I've forgotten this person's name, quickly introduce yourself to them before I'm expected to do so.' Unfortunately this ploy didn't work so well in her latter years as her husband's memory was now almost as bad as hers, so he kept forgetting what the signal meant. Perhaps Ephron should have resorted to Henry Blofeld's method of calling everyone 'my dear old thing' – the cricket commentator only came up with his catchphrase because he couldn't remember people's names.

> Charles Darwin wasn't much of a one for parties – he could only stand half an hour of conversation at a time, as it exhausted him. Clement Attlee was even more taciturn: as Tony Benn put it, *'people say conversation is supposed to be like a game of tennis, but with Attlee it was like tossing biscuits to a dog.'*

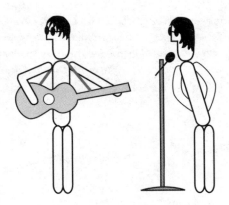

Sometimes you need to disguise your partying and its effects. Noel Gallagher says that the only difference between him and his brother Liam is that *'I don't get caught'*. Keith Richards says that the secret of walking around a corner when you're drunk is to *'never move your back away from the wall.'* On the set of *Doctor Faustus* Richard Burton's hands shook so much that in one scene where he was served tea the cup had to be glued to the saucer to prevent the rattling being picked up by microphones.

In India the Maharani (wife of the Maharaja) of Darbhanga found a clever way of getting around the ban on alcohol being consumed in her palace. She had a Rolls-Royce specially adapted to include a bar in the back, together with a seat for her lady-in-waiting to sit on and serve her. In the evening she would go out for drives and consume her gin. Unfortunately there was only one short stretch of paved road in Darbhanga – so the Maharani ordered her chauffeur to drive up and down it repeatedly.

Roger Taylor was once asked why Queen's parties were so legendary. He replied simply: *'Because we spend the most money.'*

Publilius Syrus (1st century BC Roman writer): *'If you would live innocently, seek solitude.'* Worried this might stop you from partying? Go for a compromise from Bernie Katz, who runs London's Groucho Club: *'Nothing good ever comes from staying out later than 4.00 a.m.'*

Aren't you . . . ?

It's tricky to relax in public when you're famous. The hassle of being recognised has prompted Michael Caine to don dark glasses and a baseball cap in public (it works *'until I ask for a newspaper'*), while Bruce Forsyth dislikes having his golf interrupted: *'I sign about a hundred autographs on little pads before I go out, and keep these ready in my hip pocket or golf bag. I then line the waiting people up and hand the pages out like sweeties.'*

Placido Domingo: *'If somebody asks me for an autograph, I say: "Yes, but let's walk, because if I stop maybe someone else will come up to me."'*

Marilyn Monroe once went out with a friend, who was amazed that the star wasn't getting recognised. *'It's because I'm not doing the walk,'* replied Monroe. To prove her point she launched into the hip-wiggling gait, and was instantly mobbed. When she wanted the attention, she would sometimes wear one heel lower than the other to exaggerate 'the walk'. Elvis Presley, by contrast, was persuaded of the need to do the 1968 TV special that relaunched his career when he walked down an LA street and no one came up to him.

Katharine Hepburn had a sign outside her house in Fenwick, Connecticut, saying 'Please go away', while Derren Brown shaves off his goatee between spells of work to avoid being recognised.

Another option is to become so famous that people can't believe they're seeing you. Then they'll freeze and you'll be left in peace. In the early 1990s **Dave Stewart** went for a walk with his friend **Bob Dylan** through London's Camden Market. No one came up to them – instead they stopped, open-mouthed, and pointed, as if they simply couldn't believe that Dylan was there. It was *'like walking with a ghost'*, said Stewart later.

As Chancellor of the Exchequer, Alastair Darling always bought his own groceries so he could do what he calls the 'Tesco test'. *'I make a point of watching how people react when I go shopping. If they look away, you are in trouble.'*

Janet Street-Porter: *'I want real friends, not cyberfriends. There's a Janet Street-Porter appreciation society on Facebook. They can fuck off for a start.'*

Downtime that should be uptime

It's all very well relaxing when you should be relaxing – but what about relaxing when you should be working? Should you feel guilty? You could hide behind humour, like Jerome K. Jerome: *'I like work: it fascinates me. I can sit and look at it for hours.'*

Or Douglas Adams: *'I love deadlines. I especially like the whooshing sound they make as they go flying by.'*

But there are more substantial justifications for skiving. One is a phrase used by, among others, John Lennon and Bertrand Russell, but which was coined by the writer Marthe Troly-Curtin in her 1912 book *Phrynette Married*: *'Time you enjoy wasting is not wasted time.'*

A more subtle version of the same sentiment is expressed by the writer and ex-professional cricketer Ed Smith. He was often told during his sporting career that spending time on distractions would jeopardise his on-field performance. *'But my experience suggested otherwise . . . My two best seasons were 2003, when I was writing a book, and 1997, when I was studying for my Tripos exams at Cambridge. The writing helped the batting. I was less anxious, freer, more instinctive – more amateur, if you like. By contrast, one winter in Australia I gave up all distractions apart from batting. The results were striking: I didn't get any runs.'*

Luiz Felipe Scolari, who coached Brazil's footballers to victory in the 2002 World Cup, takes the same approach: *'My priority is to ensure that players feel more amateur than professional. Thirty years ago, the effort was the other way. Now there is so much professionalism, we have to revert to urging players to like the game, love it, do it with joy.'*

A practical demonstration of how getting away from your sport can improve your performance came from the late snooker player Paul Hunter. In the 2004 Masters final at Wembley, he was 6–2 down against Ronnie O'Sullivan after the afternoon session. He went back to his hotel room with his girlfriend, indulged in a session of what he termed 'Plan B' – then came back for the evening session and won the match 10–9.

Home and dry

It's said to be where the heart is — maybe home is where the key to success lies, too . . . ?

The writer John Mortimer said he *'only ever received one piece of advice which has effectively influenced my life.'* When he was seven he locked himself into the lavatory at the Negresco Hotel in Nice, and had to be rescued by a carpenter. *'The hotel manager said to me: "Let this be a lesson to you, my boy — never lock a lavatory door for the rest of your life." And I never have.'*

Mark Twain had a billiards room at the top of his house, which was out of bounds to his wife and children: *'There ought to be a room in this house to swear in. It's dangerous to have to repress an emotion like that . . . Under certain circumstances, profanity provides a relief denied even to prayer.'*

Winston Churchill's bedroom at Chartwell was always maintained at exactly 74 degrees Fahrenheit.

Tony Iommi of Black Sabbath was asked why he lived in the Midlands rather than in LA: *'I lived there for five years but I missed sarcasm.'*

> Quentin Crisp: *'Never keep up with the Joneses. Drag them down to your level. It's cheaper.'*

The other half

Robert Harris says the secret of a good marriage is to never discuss it.

Both **Charlie Watts** and **Michael Caine** say that the secret of a long marriage is separate bathrooms. Peter Cook took it further – he and his third wife lived in separate houses on the same street; he remarked that if more people could afford to do it they would. His wife nevertheless trained him domestically, for example to use towel rails. Previously Cook had left towels on the floor. But at least they were just wet; Robert Maxwell would wipe his backside on handtowels, then leave them for his staff to pick up.

Eric Idle agrees about separate spaces: he and his wife of over 30 years have separate rooms. *'I don't mean not having sex – you can shag anywhere. I think Virginia Woolf's A Room of One's Own applies to all human beings at all stages.'*

Olivia Harrison says that being married to an ex-Beatle was tough at times, as George always got lots of attention from women. There were rocky patches in their relationship. *'So when people ask me what's the secret of a long marriage I say, "you don't get divorced".'*

Ozzy Osbourne on why he and Sharon have been married for so long. *'I'm still very much in love with Sharon. It's no more complicated than that. Having said that, when you've been on a 40-year-long bender, your memory tends to suffer, so cheating isn't a practical option. It's all very well when a natural-born con man decides to play a few away-games. If I tried it, I'd forever be in the wrong house at the wrong time, calling some poor woman by the wrong name.'*

Charles Darwin agonised over whether to get married at all. He once wrote a list headed *'This is the Question'*, with two columns headed *'Marry'* and *'Not Marry'*. The former included *'constant companion . . . who will feel interest in one, object to be beloved & played with – better than a dog anyhow.'* He also appreciated the *'charms of music and female chit-chat'* as *'good for one's health – but terrible loss of time.'* The first item in the 'Not Marry' column was: *'Not forced to visit relatives, & to bend in every trifle'*. In the end he decided to marry, but solved the relative-visiting problem by choosing as his wife his first cousin Emma.

If Clementine Churchill had anything of importance to say to her husband Winston, she put it in writing. This way she could avoid provoking an argument or being ignored altogether. The written word also played a happier role in the couple's relationship; when apart they penned four letters a day to each other.

Agatha Christie: 'Marry an archaeologist. The older you get, the more interested he is in you.'

Antoine de Saint-Exupery (author of *The Little Prince*): 'Love is not just looking at each other, it's looking in the same direction.'

Robert A. Heinlein (American science fiction writer): *'Women and cats will do as they please, and men and dogs should relax and get used to the idea.'*

Of course before any of this makes sense you have to find a partner in the first place. When it came to wooing a woman, the German playboy **Gunter Sachs** didn't do things by halves. Determined to ensnare Brigitte Bardot in the 1960s, he first took her to Monte Carlo, won £30,000 in a casino and gave it to her. Then he started delivering 100 red roses to her every day. Still unsuccessful, he took to dropping the roses from a helicopter into the garden of her beach house in St Tropez. Finally he jumped from the helicopter into the sea and swam ashore with a couple of suitcases. Bardot gave in and married him.

Travel tips: getting around

Kate Adie: *'I'd always travelled with a very small bag, from the very first trip I made abroad, worried that a large suitcase would suggest to the all-male crews that a woman needed to bring the kitchen sink along – only to discover that it's men who can't pack and therefore tote immense amounts of luggage. Women stuff shoes with make-up bottles and squeeze underwear into corners; men sit forcefully on cases . . . [I] can attest that only men insist on packing shoe-trees and hangers, that they have not mastered the art of folding anything, and always have a bag of dirty washing at the end of the trip which is mysteriously extra to what they brought.'*

Hans Christian Andersen always took a coil of rope to any hotel he stayed in, in case of fire.

Queen Victoria became a great fan of rail travel – subject to certain conditions. The Royal train was forbidden to travel at more than 40mph (or 30mph at night), and had to stop completely when the monarch ate. She refused to allow electric light, preferring oil lamps and candles (though she did permit an electric bell for summoning servants). The top layer of coal in the tender had to be whitewashed to avoid black dust offending her gaze. The industrial West Midlands upset her too – when travelling between Birmingham and Wolverhampton, Victoria would draw the blinds.

Winston Churchill only travelled on the London Underground once. This is once more than Terry Wogan.

Enrico Caruso would never start a journey on a Tuesday or a Friday.

Dean Martin always bought two seats on any plane journey he took – he didn't like to feel boxed in by another passenger.

Peter Sellers, on the other hand, always liked having someone to travel with. Persuading his friend Graham Stark to join him sometimes proved difficult – Stark was himself a successful actor. Sellers soon learned how to play it. *'The more casual the call,'* said Stark, *'the more significant the matter in hand. The theory seemed to be that if the approach was sufficiently nonchalant, the less chance there was of rejection. Eventually this nonchalance paid dividends, as human nature usually dislikes the over-eager approach, and Peter finally perfected the "couldn't care less" attitude.'*

The eighteenth-century American explorer Daniel Boone: *'I have never been lost, but I will admit to being confused for several weeks.'*

Despite not having a driving licence, the Rolling Stones drummer **Charlie Watts** has a collection of vintage cars. He likes to sit in them in the garage and listen to the engine running (though he never revs it). He even has suits tailored to match the colour scheme of each car so he can dress appropriately.

Martin Sheen listens to a Los Angeles classical music station on his car radio. If Mozart is on he'll drive past his destination rather than miss the end of the piece.

LA limo drivers mock **Robert de Niro**'s unwillingness to tip by calling him *'No Dinero'*.

John Lennon's Rolls-Royce was once mobbed by Beatles fans. The chauffeur asked if he should get the fans off the car. *'No,'* said Lennon. *'They bought it, they can wreck it.'*

LOOKING BACK ON IT ALL

And now the end is near . . . When a career is over, when a life is winding down – what's it all been about? What lessons can we learn from those who have travelled most of the road? What nuggets of wisdom are nestling in their pockets, ready to be handed down to the next generation?

The right frame of mind

'Nothing can stop the man with the right mental attitude from achieving his goal; nothing on earth can help the man with the wrong mental attitude.'
Thomas Jefferson

'No one can make you feel inferior without your consent.'
Eleanor Roosevelt

'Don't wait for the Last Judgment. It happens every day.' Albert Camus

'To conquer fear is the beginning of wisdom.'
Bertrand Russell

'It is not the mountain we conquer but ourselves.' Edmund Hillary

Slogability

As Anton Chekhov said: *'Any idiot can face a crisis; it is this day-to-day living that wears you out.'* But how should we respond when the daily grind lives up to its name? Perhaps Ernest Hemingway had the best response: *'The world breaks everyone, and afterward, some are strong at the broken places.'*

And how did Hemingway suggest we achieve that strength? *'Work every day. No matter what has happened the day or night before, get up and bite on the nail.'* Winston Churchill expressed the same sentiment in typically forthright fashion: *'Never, never, never, never ever give up!'*

Talking specifically about his own profession, Churchill once summed up the qualities you needed to survive as a politician: *'The ability to foretell what is going to happen tomorrow, next week, next month and next year. And to have the ability afterwards to explain why it didn't happen.'*

Liza Minnelli's tip for getting through a difficult time is to concentrate simply on getting through the next 15 seconds. *'Sometimes I can't even do that. So I get to 13 and say "good morning" and start my day all over again. It works. Remember: 13. I think 10 is for pussies and 15 is too long.'*

The sporting life

Damon Hill: *'Winning is everything. The only ones who remember you when you come second are your wife and your dog.'*

But listen also to one of Hill's predecessors as Formula One World Champion, Jackie Stewart: *'To finish first, first you must finish.'*

According to cricket legend Richie Benaud, captaincy is 90% luck and 10% skill. *'But don't try it without that 10%.'*

People skills

'*The most important single ingredient in the formula of success,*' said Theodore Roosevelt, '*is knowing how to get along with people.*' One way of achieving this was spelled out by the eighteenth-century British statesman Lord Chesterfield. '*Be wiser than other people if you can. But do not tell them so.*'

It took a cat to teach Florence Nightingale how to deal with people: '*I learned the lesson of life from a little kitten, one of two. The old cat comes in and says, "What are you doing here, I want my missus to myself." The bigger kitten runs away. The little one stands her ground, and when the old enemy comes near, kisses his nose and makes the peace. That is the lesson of life: kiss your enemy's nose while standing your ground.*'

Happy talk

The Victorian politician **Lord Rosebery** set himself three life targets while still at university: to marry an heiress, to own a racehorse that won the Derby, and to be Prime Minister. He achieved all three – but the last one was a disappointment. '*There are two supreme pleasures in life,*' he said later. '*One is ideal, the other real. The ideal is when a man receives the seals of office from his Sovereign. The real pleasure comes when he hands them back.*'

The Hollywood actor Rob Lowe notes that this disenchantment with success is a common characteristic of his fellow alcoholics. *'We call it the Peggy Lee Syndrome. You reach a goal you've been striving for, only to feel "Is that all there is?"'*

The solution? Aim for the state of mind summed up by Dale Carnegie: *'Success is getting what you want. Happiness is wanting what you get.'*

Age-old problems

Getting old: you can't stop it happening. So how should you deal with it?

Alan Ayckbourn: *'The only thing for old age is a brave face, a good tailor and comfortable shoes.'*

Sir Edward Grey: *'I am getting to an age when I can only enjoy the last sport left. It is called hunting for your spectacles.'*

Tom Baker: *'The older I get, the older old is.'*

Ashley Montagu: *'The idea is to die young, as late as possible.'*

Patrick Moore: *'I get my daily paper, look at the obituaries page and if I'm not there I carry on as usual.'*

Oscar Wilde: *'The old believe everything; the middle-aged suspect everything; the young know everything.'*

Helen Mirren: *'The day you're born, an old person starts off on a journey, and one day they're going to knock at the door and you'll open it to them. And there you are!'*

The comedian Bob Monkhouse pointed out that: *'Growing old is compulsory, growing up is optional.'* But Pablo Picasso reminded us that maturity doesn't have to mean losing touch completely with your inner child. Indeed for some professions it's vital that you don't: *'Every child is born an artist. The trouble is how to stay one as you grow up.'*

Death becomes you

The final question in this book is the final question in life – how should you approach its end? When the grim reaper comes calling, how will you reply? Listen for a minute to the words of Walter Breuning, who died, on 14 April 2011, as the world's oldest man. Asked how he had reached the grand old age of 114, he listed a number of tips:

embrace change, even when it seems for the worse – *'every change is good'*

eat two meals a day – *'that's all you need'*

work as long as you can – *'that money's going to come in handy'*

But Breuning's most important piece of advice came from his grandfather: accept death. **'We're going to die,'** he said. **'Some people are scared of dying. Never be afraid to die. Because you're born to die.'**

And when you're gone? If you find immortality unappealing, you could follow the example of John Keats, who decreed that his name should not appear on his grave. Instead it says **'here lies one whose name was writ in water'**, and Keats is referred to simply as **'a young English poet'**.

And if you do want to be remembered, how about ensuring that it's with a smile? The inventor of the Pringles tube had his ashes buried in . . . a Pringles tube. The broadcaster Alistair Cooke wanted his ashes scattered in his beloved Central Park in New York. This is forbidden – so his friends and family collected some empty cups from a Starbucks just round the corner, and used them to smuggle the ashes into the park. They formed a circle, recited a psalm and said a prayer of thanks for Cooke's life – then each scattered their allotted portion of the great man to the wind.

Elizabeth Taylor left everyone laughing. Her funeral service, at Forest Lawn cemetery in Glendale, California, was scheduled to begin at 2.00 p.m. But in accordance with Taylor's instructions it actually began 15 minutes later, with the announcement: **'She even wanted to be late for her own funeral.**